MONDRIAN

Nature to Abstraction

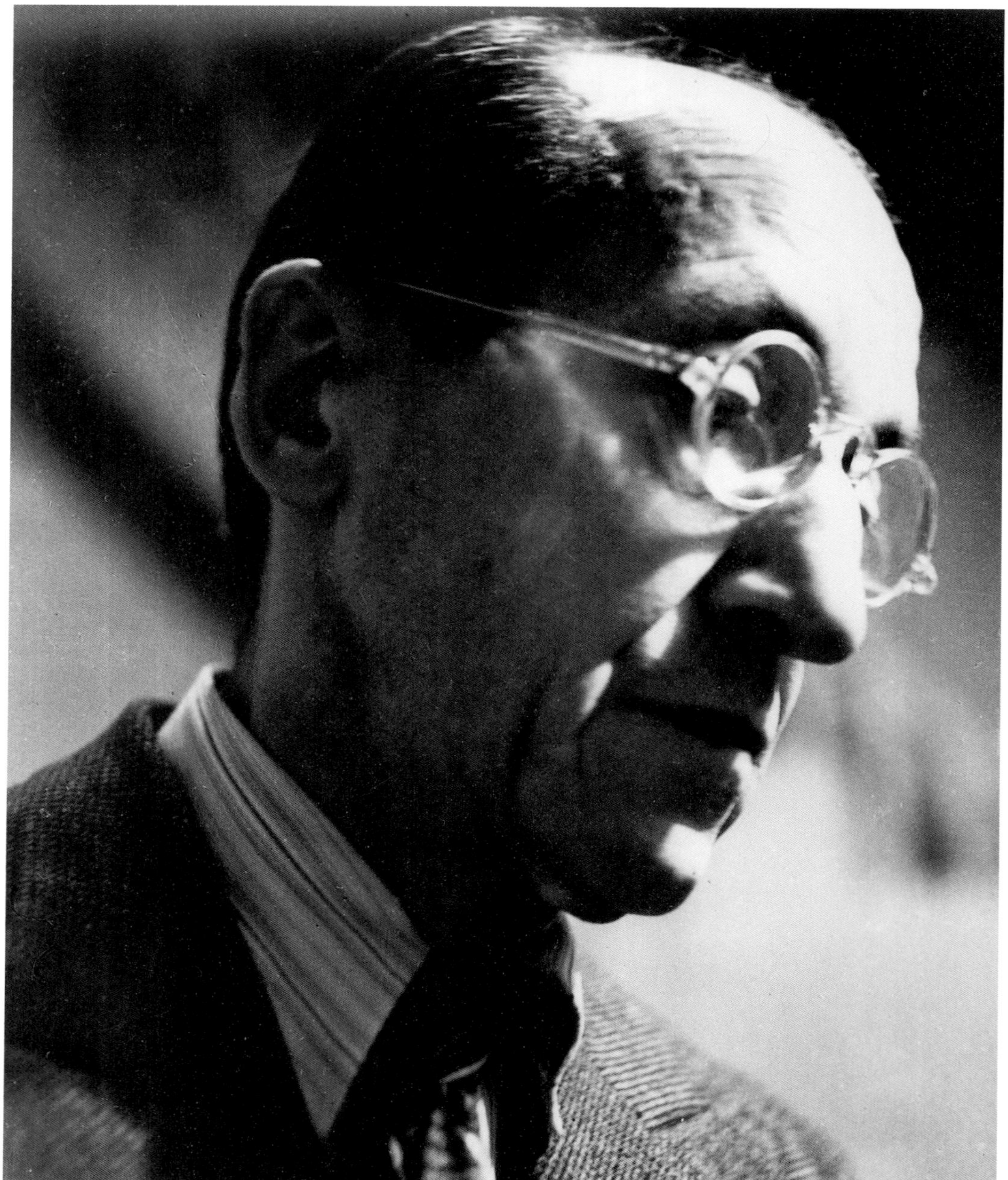

BRIDGET RILEY

MONDRIAN

Nature to Abstraction

From the Gemeentemuseum, The Hague

TATE GALLERY PUBLISHING

Exhibition sponsored by AT&T

AT&T

Front cover:
Composition of Lines and Colour III: Composition with Blue 1937 (cat.70)

Back cover:
Forest 1898–1900 (cat.1)

Frontispiece:
Piet Mondrian, *c.*1934–6

ISBN 1 85437 237 8
A catalogue record for this publication is available from the British Library

Published by order of the Trustees
to accompany the exhibition at the Tate Gallery
26 July – 30 November 1997

Published by Tate Gallery Publishing Limited
Millbank, London SW1P 4RG

Designed and typeset by Caroline Johnston
Printed and bound in Great Britain by
Balding + Mansell, Norwich

CONTENTS

SPONSOR'S FOREWORD

AT&T is pleased to be sponsoring the Tate Gallery's exhibition *Mondrian: Nature to Abstraction*. A key figure in the development of abstract art, Mondrian exemplified innovation and the essence of change in artistic expression. This particular exhibition provides a rare glimpse of how Mondrian's experience with naturalism influenced his later works, demonstrating the nature of evolution and growth.

Like Mondrian, AT&T is a leader in furthering the benefits of communication with the goal of providing people with new and better ways to communicate. As a global communications and information services company, AT&T strives to ensure that its customers, both businesses and consumers and the communities in which we operate can have immediate access to the tools and the solutions needed to grow and prosper.

Today, we operate the world's largest, most sophisticated communications network, serving more than ninety million businesses and consumer customers. In the UK, our presence in the marketplace is strong and continues to grow. Our aim in the UK is to provide our customers with a better choice for their communications needs, together with meaningful support of the arts, cultural and educational efforts of the community. We hope this will enable us all to look with vision towards a brighter future.

Jennifer Samuel
Communications Director
AT&T (UK) Ltd

FOREWORD

Last autumn the Haags Gemeentemuseum kindly offered to lend the Tate a selection from its extensive collection of works by Mondrian during a period in which their museum was closed for renovation. We accepted with alacrity and eagerness, being aware that more than forty years have passed since the last significant Mondrian exhibition in London, presented at the Whitechapel Art Gallery by Bryan Robertson. It was an opportunity not to be missed and we are really delighted that a British public should be able to see this remarkable collection.

The choice of works was to be ours and we asked the artist Bridget Riley to assist, knowing her great admiration for Mondrian. We are immensely grateful to her for devoting so much time to the show and for her immense enthusiasm for the project.

Bridget Riley made the selection in collaboration with Sean Rainbird, Assistant Keeper of the Modern Collection at the Tate Gallery, advised and helped by Hans Janssen, Head of the Department of Modern Art at the Gemeentemuseum.

The Haags Gemeentemuseum's Mondrian collection is richest in early work and we have therefore added a few later paintings both from our own collection and from other sources, to give a better balance to a survey of Mondrian's achievement. We should like to offer our sincere thanks to the lenders of these additional works who so generously agreed to lend at rather short notice.

We are deeply grateful to Dr J.L. Locher, Director of the Haags Gemeentemuseum, for his great generosity and to his many colleagues for their cooperation. I should particularly like to thank Hans Janssen who has been tremendously supportive throughout. He, too, has shown great enthusiasm and excitement at the thought of Mondrian at the Tate and we are most grateful to him for everything he and his colleagues have done to make the organisation of the project run so smoothly.

Finally we offer our sincere thanks to AT&T whose generous funding has helped make this presentation possible. We are delighted to welcome them back to the Tate following their successful sponsorship of the David Hockney exhibition in 1988.

Nicholas Serota
Director

MONDRIAN PERCEIVED

Bridget Riley

An artist's early work is inevitably made up of a mixture of tendencies and interests, some of which are compatible and some of which are in conflict with each other. As the artist picks his way, rejecting and accepting as he goes, certain patterns of enquiry emerge. His failures are as valuable as his successes in that by misjudging one thing he confirms something else, even if at the time he does not know what that something else is. In that sense, although Mondrian may sometimes fail, he never makes mistakes, everything in his development is of use and contributes to that development.

There are two conflicting traits in his temperament, in the sense given to the word by Baudelaire and Cézanne – 'temperament' as an artist's own particular and ineradicable nature. One is a feeling for rhythm, which quickens to the pulse of life and seems somehow to be connected with his positive sense of the new; and the other, a love of order and balance, which is at the root of his search for unity and fullness. Both these traits can also have an obverse side: the lively quality may lead to an extreme dynamism and fragmentation, while the insistence on order can sometimes turn into a bland and almost schematic statement. These two temperamental qualities ebb and flow throughout the various preoccupations and styles of his development – one now in ascendancy, and then the other, until they slowly find a resolution in the late abstract works.

The early landscapes painted in Holland are predominantly tonal in treatment and have a low-key, moody character. Trees and buildings reflected in water produce self-contained symmetrical images which cut recession short and pull the field of vision up close. Evening light is frequently chosen and there is a marked interest in visual phenomena bordering on the apparitional. The tree in *Evening on the Gein* 1906 (cat.9), far from calling on natural similitude, looms over the dark shape of the river bank and its reflection like some ominous sign; and in *Trees on the Gein: Moonrise* 1907–8 (cat.14) the five trees are treated as a spectral frieze spread flat against the light of the moon.

This up-closeness is carried further in a choice of subjects in which the sense of an unencompassable presence and an overpowering scale dominate. In his *Trialogue* (1910–12) Mondrian, under the guise of the 'abstract realist painter', says about *Red Mill* 1910–11 (cat.33): 'Indeed I find this windmill very beautiful, particularly now that we are too close to view it in normal perspective and therefore cannot see it or draw it normally. From here, it is very difficult merely to reproduce what one sees.'[1] The final painting conveys the sensation of something grand towering up above the spectator's viewpoint.

The recurrent subject of sea, sky and dunes provides a theme of vast, uncentred openness. The lack of differentiation in such motifs gives a singular prominence to the horizon line and its reverberations. By stacking and interlocking horizontal divisions of different weights and distances Mondrian creates a fluctuating, impalpable envelope of space.

From very early on there seems to have been a special attraction to trees and to the pictorial problem of how branches, sky and foliage or blossom interact and interpenetrate. Being essentially a subject that cannot be treated 'realistically', the tree offers a marvellous pretext for the fabrication of a rhythmic structure of shallow recessions and advances that have little or nothing to do with the void and solid of the original motif. The potential of this subject was to be most fully realised in Mondrian's Cubist work.

But before that Mondrian discovered colour. It first entered his world through van Gogh and Divisionism. Both the vibrancy of autonomous brushwork and the abstract intensity of colour contrast must have appealed to his feeling for rhythm and dynamism. In *Red Tree* 1908 (cat.17) the sensation of evening light has shed its moody aura and Mondrian fairly crackles the painting into life with equivalents of red and blue and short energetic brushmarks. From there it is only a small shift to the liberation of colour from any descriptive or representational function. This Fauvist approach can be seen in *Mill in Sunlight* of the same year (cat.19). The dazzling heat and light of a midsummer day is recast in stabbing strokes and blotches of red and yellow shot through with pale blue and violet.

But Mondrian's development is not simply one of a young painter finding out what to paint and how to paint it. Like van Gogh, he comes from a Dutch background deeply involved with religious matters, and in a similar way his fulfilment as an artist is inseparably connected with transforming these roots. The parallel is striking because it shows that even a cultural basis as alien and unsympathetic to artistic aspiration as fervent Protestantism is not necessarily an obstacle. It is a question of whether an artist is strong enough to turn this predicament to advantage. Van Gogh was able to transform his religious zeal and empathy with the people working in the coal mines into preaching a virtual gospel of the power of the sun. Whereas Mondrian, who initially engaged in Theosophy and all sorts of attempts to reconcile philosophical speculation with Christianity, had to discover in the basic properties of painting the means that allowed him to fulfil his spiritual quest.

The crucial painting in this context is *Evolution* 1910–11 (cat.31). It is something of an embarrassment to many people who love Mondrian as an abstract purist; and for those who claim that Mondrian is a symbolist and not really an abstract artist at all, this painting serves as the basic reference point. In fact it deserves neither of these responses. It is a unique and revealing failure on an imaginative scale only comparable to Cézanne's early expressive works such as the *Eternal Feminin* and the *New Olympia*. No fashionable or well-behaved artist would ever dare risk something like this; it takes an unselfconscious and uncompromising imagination to go to such awkward lengths. Over and above its obvious pictorial shortcomings the failure of the work is objective. In *Evolution* Mondrian attempts to make a universal statement about life – a task of a dimension traditionally only accomplished through the agency of Biblical subjects and Antique mythology. The fact that this whole sphere of representation was no longer available had been an essential mainspring in the formation of Modern art in the nineteenth century. Mondrian had to discover for himself that literary symbolism and personal invention could not make up for this loss. The creation of a common social language does not lie within the scope of an individual and the lack of such a basis has to be accepted by Modern painting.

It would have been almost impossible for a young artist to deal with this gigantic problem on his own, particularly when living in a provincial context. Soon after *Evolution* was completed Mondrian left for Paris where, through the daring and brilliance of its pioneers, the Modern movement had already begun to make its response to this crisis. Just as van Gogh had found liberation in the Divisionist approach to colour that nineteenth-century Paris offered him, so Mondrian, following a similar pattern of emancipation, found a key to spatial organisation through Cubism in twentieth-century Paris. However, as some contemporary critics observed, his interpretation of Cubism was clearly very much his own. His work was recognised for being 'extremely original in conception' (Leo Faust) and for the mark that it bore of temperamental distinction, while his complete indifference to the Cubist 'laws of volume' (André Salmon) – that is to say the remarkable flatness of his paintings – drew the criticism of other reviewers.

In Paris Mondrian worked first from the lattice-like drawings of trees done previously in Holland and then from small diagrammatic notes he made of the planes of interior walls exposed in the demolition of large houses near his studio. These walls bore the remnants of the wallpaper and paint that had once decorated rooms on each floor and presented patches of colour placed haphazardly on a flat surface. Both motifs were treated close up, filling the visual field, and provided Mondrian with a loose, informal grid within which he could articulate planes of subdued colours: the warm-cold binaries of classic Cubism, his own lightly coloured greys, or muted shades of red, yellow and blue. Ultimately the two aspects of his Cubist paintings that were to prove most important to the development of his later abstract work were the dynamic relationships of these areas within the picture plane and the new role assigned to the spectator in assessing these relationships. That is to say, the way in which we 'read' the paintings is a constituent part of their formation.

Within a few years Mondrian had absorbed influences from three seminal movements of Modern art – Divisionism, Fauvism and Cubism. The impact was clearly very strong. To sort out this experience he needed time, and reduced exposure to the Parisian art scene. He returned to Holland for the summer 1914, and when the War broke out in August was unable to return to Paris until 1919 when it was over. This enforced break enabled him to take stock; to reflect on the various phases and changes that had taken place in his work, and gradually to find his own footing with greater certainty. In 1915 he made a distinction between the human spirit in its role as a builder within the realities of an artistic medium and the 'moody' quality of emotion with its expressive dependence on external reality: 'Emotion is more outward than spirit. Spirit constructs, composes; emotion expresses mood and the like. Spirit constructs most purely, with the simplest line and the most basic colour.'

In Holland Mondrian at first continued with the façade motifs, now based on the church at Domburg, but the dunes and the sea soon exerted their pull. We have a friend's account of strolling with Mondrian on the beach: 'On a walk beside the ocean, late in the evening, under a radiant, starry sky, he took a tiny sketchbook out of his pocket and made a scribbled drawing of a starry night. For days he worked over that suggestive little scribble. Every day he took a tiny step further away from reality and came a tiny step nearer to the spiritual evocation of it' (autumn 1914). This gradual shift from an emotional response to a spiritual realisation gave rise to the beautiful series of preparatory drawings leading up to *Pier and Ocean* 1915 (fig.1). In the final painting an immensity of sensation opens up; one feels oneself surrounded by the sparkling stillness and the rhythmic movement of some boundless continuum. Here Mondrian's lines take on a wider range of functions, they act as breaks, points and accents. At one stage in the development of *Pier and Ocean* Mondrian thought of adding colour, but in the end decided against it. However, in the very next painting, *Composition 1916* (fig.2), he did precisely that. A pervasive grey with red, yellow and blue patches – sometimes light, sometimes darker, but always adjusted – support and contradict the beats, crosses and intervals of the lines.

Slowly the work loosens its moorings in what Mondrian refers to as 'given in Nature' and begins to make its way autonomously. Colour planes are simply arranged on a white ground, grey lines are added to provide a context for the spatial movement of these planes without destroying their dynamism. The introduction of regular grids was strongly objected to by friends such as van Doesburg for being repetitious and denying composition; but Mondrian defended them on the grounds that he reworks the regular division considerably, and in the case of the *Chequerboard* paintings he maintained that he achieves contrast through the weight and disposition of his colour planes. However, he also had reservations about this direction, as he later admitted, for being too 'vague': 'The verticals and horizontals cancelled each other; the result was confused, the structure was lost.'

During this period in Holland Mondrian wrote and published *The New Plastic in Painting* (1917) in which he sets forth his criteria. Part speculative thinking, part soliloquy, and part reverie, this book has done almost as much to confuse as to enlighten his followers. However, although it does not provide a complete framework with all its reference points in place, the expressions and definitions Mondrian uses offer important clues in themselves. One gets nearer to the nature of his endeavour by starting from these basic terms than by trying to grasp an overall system or find a comprehensive theory.

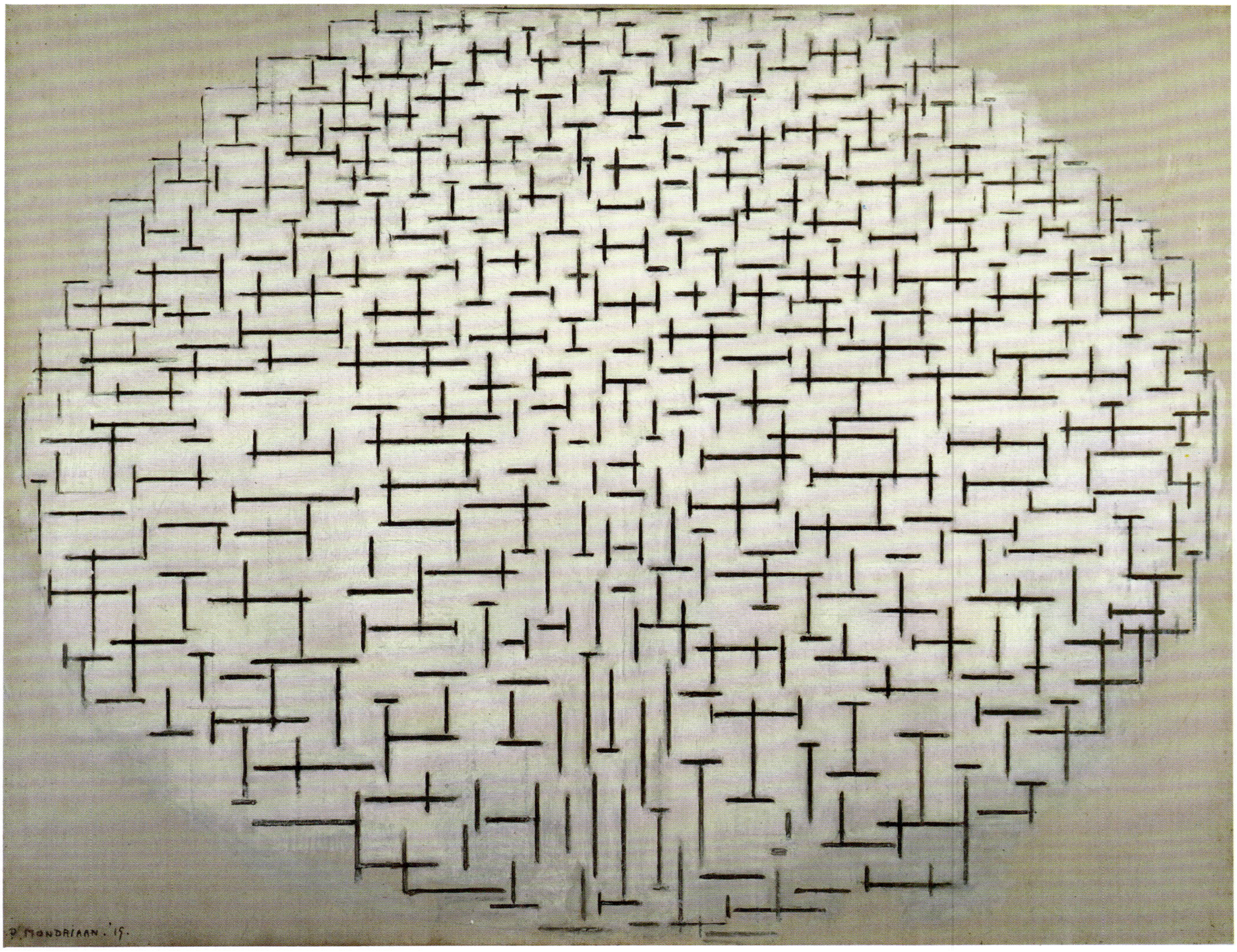

fig.1

Composition 10 in Black and White: Pier and Ocean

1915, oil on canvas 85 × 108 cm. Kröller-Müller Museum, Otterlo

On his return to Paris in June 1919 the effects of this reflective and withdrawn period in Holland soon became apparent. Of *Composition A: Composition with Black, Red, Grey, Yellow and Blue* 1920 (fig.3), on which he worked for the best part of a year, he said: 'I have now made a painting that pleases me more than all my previous work ... It has been a long quest.' Although in the light of his classic period in the 1920s this work can be seen as transitional, it is more revealing in many ways than those highly accomplished paintings. The peculiar flatness of his pictorial space that had already been observed in his Cubist work is now developed and clarified. The colour planes take up different positions in space – some advance, some recede; and this is not a simple matter of a particular hue always taking up the same spatial position wherever present. It is a question of context. Take the three yellows for example: the yellow in the top right corner is on a different plane from the yellow in the centre, and both of these are again on different planes from the yellow in the lower right. Although one customarily thinks of yellow as a light colour, these three yellows have different visual weights – that is to say, the block in the top right appears slightly heavier than the central yellow, which in turn weighs visually more than the yellow rectangle in the lower right. These three yellows, therefore, do two principal things simultaneously: they take up different spatial planes and they exert pressures through their different weights. The same applies to the reds, the blues and blacks, and of course to the greys and whites (although there it is perhaps less easy to see). This brings about a field of forces in which the various weights and planes are building up dynamic relationships and tensions.

Such dynamism could easily lead to a sort of visual anarchy. But Mondrian practices a form of ordering that he later referred to as 'the equivalence of the dissimilar'. The disparate visual qualities – each in itself completely 'real', or as he would say 'determinate' – are balanced in such a way that they both build a whole and yet retain their individuality.[2] 'I have just got that large work right', he writes to van Doesburg about *Composition A*. 'I made that blue square on the right and changed that yellow one on the left to white; I painted over the grey, the black and the white. I wish you could have seen it like this.' And as the final result shows, he altered the painting again. In this way an 'equilibrated relationship' is achieved which, in his words, 'most purely expresses the universal, the harmony, the unity that are proper to the spirit'. So anxious was he to preserve the individual characteristics within this unity that he worried for quite a while about the intensity of the large red in the lower left of the painting: 'I am not absolutely sure that it ought to be so totally homogeneous. In theory it should be, but in practice... ?'. Eventually he decided to leave it alone.

Gradually it becomes clear that this abstract way of ordering forms the content of Mondrian's work. His paintings are not symbolic or transcendental, but perceptually accessible and plastic in the sense that he builds a structure of relationships that places us, as spectators, in an analogous 'equilibrium'. We are invited to participate in a visual interplay between weights, forces and tensions held together by a balance that is neither symmetrical

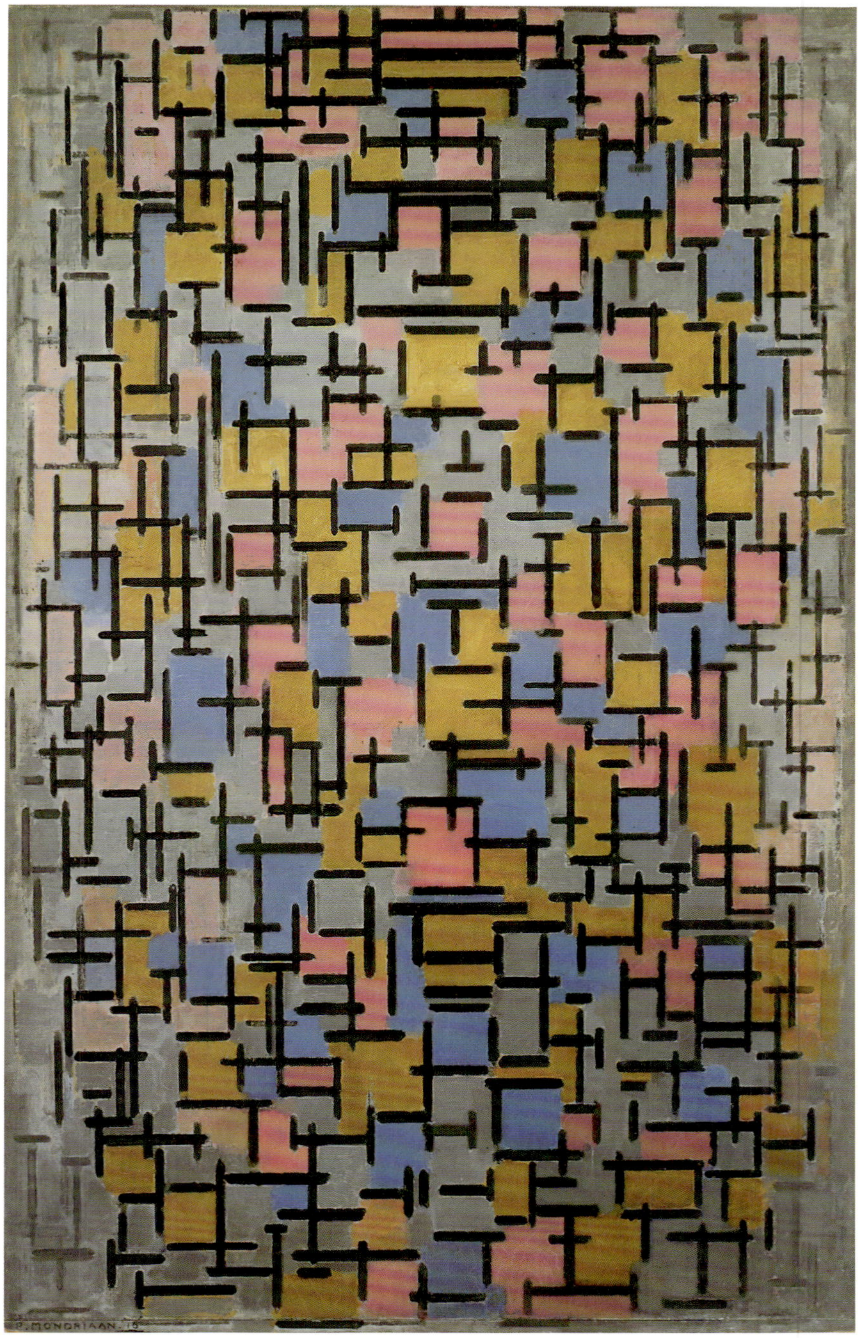

fig.2

Composition 1916

1916, oil on canvas with wood strip nailed to bottom edge
119 × 75.1 cm. Solomon R. Guggenheim Museum, New York

nor systematic. In a remarkable essay of 1923, *No Axiom but the Plastic Principle,* Mondrian describes this balancing between the individual elements and their dynamic unity as the plastic principle and purpose of his art in a period when, as he says: 'Everything is seen "relatively" … Moreover the relativity, the mutability of things creates in us a desire for the absolute, the immutable.' Far from resolving this conflict by offering a new 'absolute', he turns the in-built contradiction into a dynamic relationship that becomes something of an absolute in itself and which has to be rediscovered and re-established in each particular instance; that is to say: painting by painting. *Composition with Red, Blue, Black, Yellow and Grey* 1921 (cat.62) shows with what awesomely simple means Mondrian can achieve his objective. There is no explicit centre to the painting, and yet the peripheral events do not drift apart. With their differing characteristics they form a correlation of forces that hold the square in tension, being both open and defined at the same time.

As the body of Mondrian's mature work grew throughout the 1920s this plastic principle gave rise to a tremendous richness and variety. Quite apart from changes in the proportion of the rectangular canvases and the dramatic shift in orientation of the diamond paintings, Mondrian pursues, alongside these changes, a number of themes in the almost serial manner he had sometimes employed in the past. He may explore the weights and tensions that can hold an empty centre as in the painting just described; or the reverse, as in *Composition with Red, Black, Blue and Yellow* 1921 (cat.61), where the linear divisions cut across the central area and the visual forces are turned inside out, as it were. As a result the colour weights and planes, being well within the pictorial field, provoke relationships that concentrate or diffuse attention. Other areas of investigation include an even greater reduction of his already simplified means, such as just black bands of varying width with just white planes of varying proportion; or compositions with only one or two colour planes occupying the spatial compartments provided by the linear divisions.

For a long time this period was regarded as the zenith of Mondrian's achievement. Certainly the monumental stability and grandeur reflects one side of his temperament. However, the other, the lively feeling for rhythm, was soon to assert itself and to increase dramatically the dynamic element in his work. In 1932 he made his first 'double line' paintings, among them *Composition with Yellow and Double Line* (cat.66). The rapid repetition of the horizontal line adds a new and different quality of plane, a kind of outlined band, to the relationships in the painting – and one so subversive that it puts the stability and coherence of the painting at risk. But when, as in *Composition with Red, Yellow and Blue* 1935 (cat.67), he widens the interval between the two lines, the ambiguous duality of this new relationship is reduced and the plane thus created sits more easily with others in the painting. However, the friction of the 'double line' is there to stay, as Mondrian is obviously fascinated by its rhythmic potential and repetitive insistence. In the following year, 1936, he painted *Composition C* 1936 (cat.68). There, a centralised black vertical cuts the pictorial

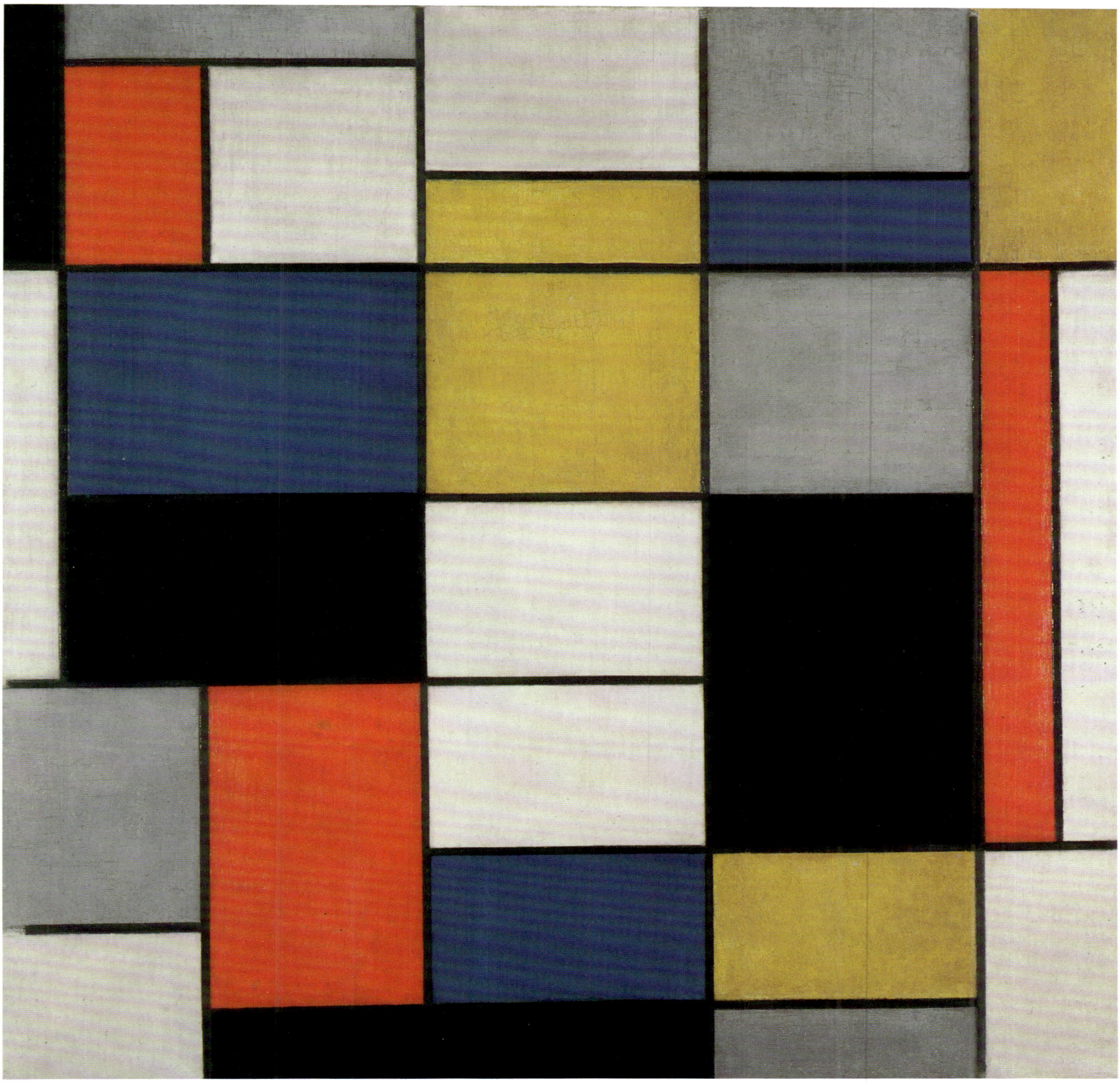

fig.3

Composition A: Composition with Black, Red, Grey, Yellow, and Blue

1920, oil on canvas 91.5 × 92 cm. Galleria Nazionale d'Arte Moderna, Rome

field in half and is repeated to the left to form a 'double line', while a pair of horizontal 'double lines' (with slightly wider but equal intervals) crosses these verticals, setting up virtual flashing points at the intersections. But now Mondrian tackles directly those aspects of repetition that perhaps seemed most problematic to him: the accumulated intensity of the overall dynamism, which threatens to diminish the 'particular' at the expense of the 'universal'. By adding a large yellow plane and a small blue one he introduces a strong asymmetrical bias that checks the evenness of the rhythm.

In 1937 – the year before he left France for England and New York – he made *Composition with Blue* (cat.70), a most beautiful painting that reconciles the increasing role he was giving to rhythm with a new sense of scale and tectonic strength. Generated by various black verticals and their intervals the movement sweeps across the painting and is brought to a complex, rhythmic close on the right. A subtle counter-movement of horizontal intervals modifies and harmonises the drive and tempo of the painting. As a finishing stroke an implied diagonal descending from the top left is pulled up for attention by the deep blue rectangle it carries, the only colour plane in the painting.

During the last few years of his life, spent in New York, Mondrian carried on with his explorations, which more and more amounted to a reversal of the priorities that had governed his work in the 1920s. In his writings and in conversation he insisted repeatedly on 'dynamic rhythm' and 'creative destruction' by which he meant the transformation of the actual elements – the basic colours and lines – into the 'purely plastic' agents of an expressive dynamism. His last completed painting, *Broadway Boogie Woogie* 1942–3 (fig.4), seems to sum up his entire endeavour in one amazing statement. Earlier tendencies such as those revealed in *Pier and Ocean*, the diamond and the *Chequerboard* paintings are integrated with interests that previously seemed to contradict and exclude them. The striving for constancy and immutability coexists with the love of rhythm and movement. It can be taken as a proof of Mondrian's rigorous and somewhat antiquated effort to achieve the 'equilibrium of the universal and the particular' that his paintings have not been rendered obsolete by history. However frail and modest their physical appearance may be, they shine among the best works of this century with a unique vitality and mysterious timelessness.

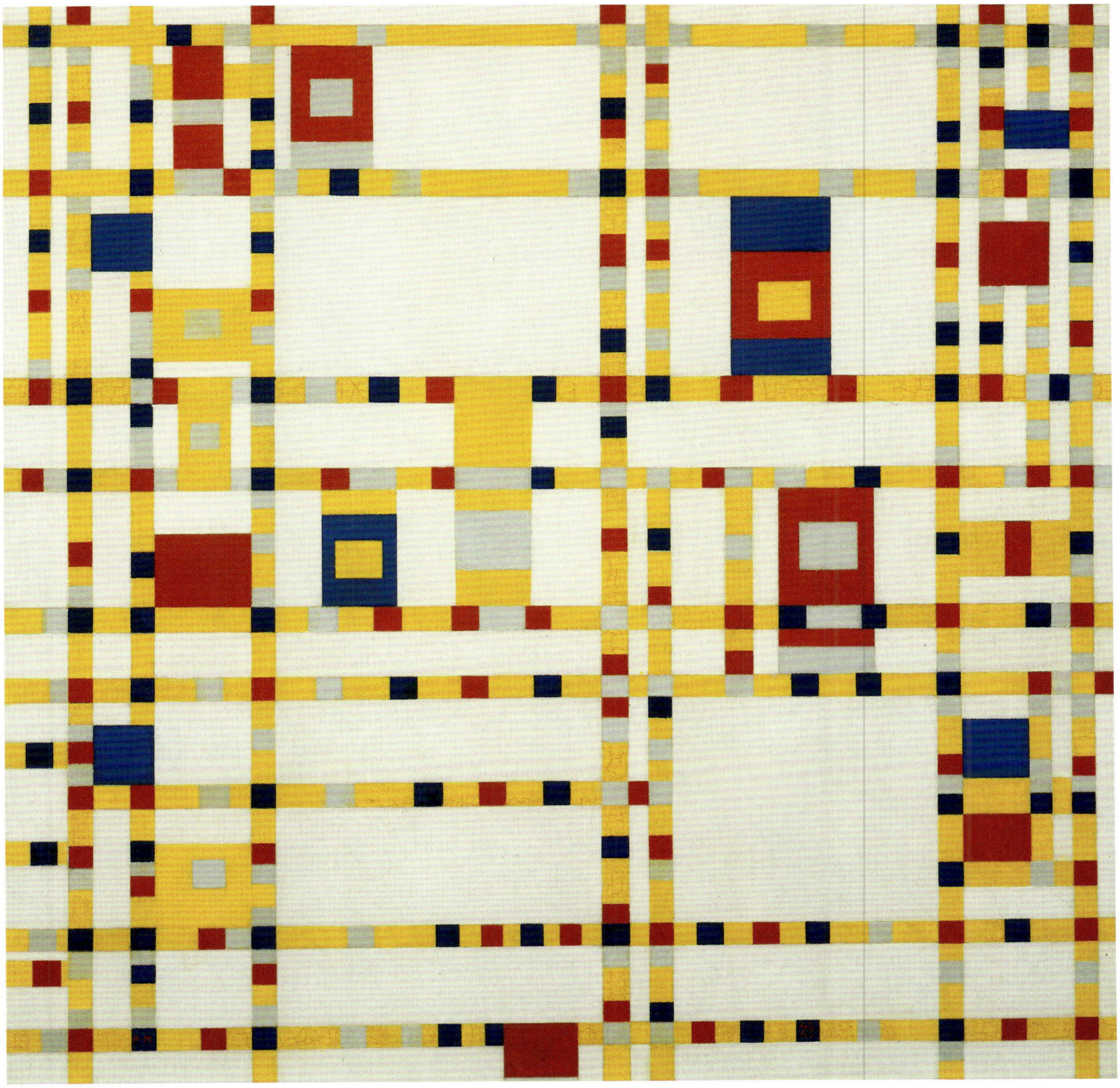

fig.4

Broadway Boogie Woogie

1942–3, oil on canvas 127 × 127 cm. The Museum of Modern Art, New York.
Given anonymously

NOTES

1 References throughout are made either to H. Holtzman and M. James, *The New Art – The New Life: The Collected Writings of Piet Mondrian*, Boston 1986, or to A. Zander Rudenstine (ed.), *Piet Mondrian*, exh. cat. The Hague, Washington and New York, 1995–6.

2 This relationship has been the subject of my paper given at a symposium on 20 November 1995, during the run of the Mondrian retrospective at the Museum of Modern Art, New York. It has been published under the title 'Mondrian: The "Universal" and the "Particular"' in *Burlington Magazine*, vol.138, no.1124, Nov. 1996, pp.751–3.

BRINGING ABOUT LIGHT

On the Function of Colour in Mondrian's Painting

Hans Janssen

Piet Mondrian's oeuvre is usually divided into two distinct parts: the early and the late works. The early Mondrian was a landscape painter whose compositions originated from a regional tradition, and although he underwent a period of transition, this phase lasted roughly until 1912 when he went to Paris and left everything behind: his early landscapes, the Dutch art world and particularly the tie between his work and nature. His contribution to Modernism marginalised the early Mondrian, and the abstract Mondrian can be regarded as more or less detached from the regionalism of his youth. This was no accident: Mondrian deliberately drove a wedge between his early landscapes and his later work, leaving the dead weight of his past behind in the Netherlands and detaching his work from his memories. Yet the Modernist paintings are closer to his earlier output than is sometimes assumed.

Yellow Lines

One of the most important paintings in the collection of the Haags Gemeentemuseum is Mondrian's *Composition with Yellow Lines* 1933 (cat.64). It is an atypical work that seriously unsettles the traditional image of the artist as a pioneer of right-angled, black line patterns and primary colour fields. The surface of the diamond-shaped canvas is smoothly painted in a clear white. The only other visual elements are four bright yellow lines, or strips, placed at right angles to each other in the corners. The yellow, contiguous to the white, stresses the subtle dissimilarity between the two colours and enhances the intensity of the white. Moreover, the yellow lines differ in width but not in relative position or length, which introduces an element of motion to the otherwise unstirring surface. The distance between the yellow lines approximately equals the square measure of the canvas, thus creating both a correspondence and a gentle contrast between the horizontal and vertical positions of the lines and the diamond shape, and bringing a dynamic element into the work's stillness. This understated contrast is echoed by the fine distinction between the yellow and the white, resulting in a radiance that is reinforced by the similarity but inequality of the lines. The receding frame, its two slats gradually sloping towards the wall and painted in the same white as the canvas, marks, and at the same time mitigates, the transition between canvas and wall. The painting is a marvel of subtlety, economy and animation. It breathes a crystalline clarity that dominates the space. Almost hieratic, the painting exemplifies light.

Composition with Yellow Lines has recently been described as the result of Mondrian's consistent sabotage of his own theoretical assumptions, a destruction of former positions guided by a plastic reflection that relies only on the visual revelation manifesting itself in visual art.[1] There is more to be observed, however, particularly with regard to the special use of colour in the painting – a direct result of issues that had occupied Mondrian much earlier in his career as an artist.

Mondrian on a bicycle

In a drawing made by Simon Maris in 1906–7 (fig.5) Mondrian, pipe in mouth, cap on head, palette and brush in hand, precariously balances on a bicycle supported by iron arches, ropes and pegs. On the handlebars is a painter's box, and in its lid there appears to be a piece of cloth or cardboard on which he is attentively at work. The drawing was executed at a time when Mondrian wanted to make his mark as a landscape painter. Not completely detached from the traditions of the Hague School, but just free enough to work in a more exalted fashion – as was the favoured style in the Amsterdam art world at this time – he conveyed his impressions in an unconventional manner within the limits of the traditional dark palette. His emphasis on the personal aesthetic experience manifested itself in dense, inflexible, sometimes extremely experimental compositions. *Ditch near the Gein* 1901–2 (cat.4), for instance, is dominated by a high horizon that barely offers space to the ditch, which is painted in flat, matt colours. The pollarded willow in the foreground enhances the flatness instead of providing depth. But the most fascinating thing about this small sketch is the dull, brackish light caused by the interplay of barely contrasting colours, moulded in solid forms.

In some of these early works Mondrian explored the spatial possibilities of detail. *Sheepfold in the Evening* 1906 (cat.11), for example, is a miracle of economy in regard to the creation of space. With closely connecting gradations of creamy yellow chalk and charcoal he conjures up an immense night space and an accompanying sense of enhanced colour. Until 1908 Mondrian browsed through the dominant traditions of the moment without adhering to any school and always in search of experiment. Critics blamed him for not pursuing the indisputable dreamy aspect of his work, the quiet beauty of lines and simple forms; he was distracted, they claimed, by weird and unconvincing colours. Years later, Mondrian himself wrote about this period: 'The first thing to change in my painting was the colour. I forsook natural colour for pure colour. I had come to feel that the colours of nature cannot be reproduced on canvas. Instinctively, I felt that painting had to find a new way to express the beauty of nature.'[2]

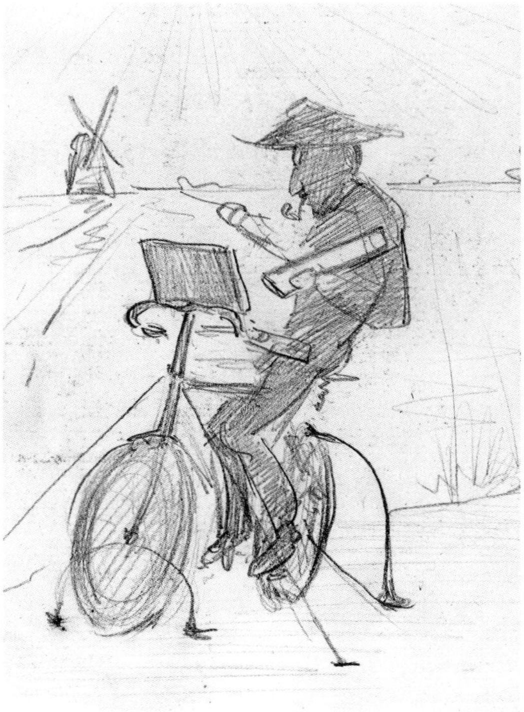

fig.5 SIMON MARIS

Mondrian Painting on a Bicycle

c.1906–7, pencil in sketchbook 12.5 × 7.9 cm. Private Collection

During the period that the drawing of the artist on his bicycle was made, Mondrian was capturing in his work the beauty of nature in colours and forms that suggested a stillness and timelessness. Though some of the early works use accents to define space, details normally present themselves as parts of a fluid process; objects blend to create big, summary forms in which colour is the dominant factor. Both colour and form are intended to reveal a meaning that is to be found in a sense of infinity and transcendence. Early in his career Mondrian had already developed the habit of treating the same motif completely differently in each work, even when the composition remained constant. This serial approach seems to betray his preference for the tension between identical motifs and their variations and puts him in the company of Modernists such as Kandinsky and Monet.[3] Carel Blotkamp has rightly linked each Mondrian series to the stages of dematerialisation connected to the cycle of nature, in which Mondrian had an interest. By stylising the design and experimenting with the visual means, Mondrian emphasised the various symbolic possibilities of a motif in order to accentuate the constant, timeless aspect of landscape. To this end, he devoted a good deal of attention to light: not the atmospheric light of the Hague School or the Impressionists, but a more subdued, intimate light such as that manifested in *Sheepfold in the Evening*.

Around 1906–7, Mondrian was known as a meditative, spiritual artist who searched in his landscapes for a visual form identical to inner nature: the space of *Sheepfold in the Evening* is ultimately a spiritual one. It was said that in these evening landscapes Mondrian was able to 'unweave the soul', meaning that the paintings emanated a contemplative, inwardly oriented effect.[4] Mondrian himself shared this view. By 1908–9 he had begun to sketch self-portraits in which he emphasised a penetrating, staring gaze. He strove after a special kind of seeing, to which he reverentially applied the mystical term *schouwen*, best translated as 'witnessing': a manner of observation that is intensely sensitive where seeing becomes an almost magic activity. Mondrian had already stepped off his bicycle.

Mill in Sunlight

The artist on his bicycle is situated in a summarily indicated, flat polder near Amsterdam. Ditches lead straight to the horizon, where a mill is standing in the blazing sunbeams, represented by pencil lines. This detail connects the small drawing to the works made around 1908 when Mondrian secured himself once and for all a position within the progressive sector of the Dutch art world with his *Mill in Sunlight* (cat. 19), the first painting to provoke critical attention. It is regarded as the pinnacle of Luminism, the movement that searched for a different light and mood through the dissection of colours and a quick, direct touch. Except for some emerald green in the lower part of the building, *Mill in Sunlight* is composed of shining red and glowing orange riddled with ultramarine and purple. The foreground is indicated by short, biting brushstrokes in yellow and ochre representing the bank of the ditch in which the mill is reflected in red, violet and blue. Using a palette knife, Mondrian sets up the sky in cadmium yellow and greyish blue. The higher their position in the painting, the more saturated and oily the colours are. At the bottom, an expressive violet predominates; at the top, primary colours prevail: the mill red and ultramarine, the sky yellow. Most critics were totally flabbergasted by the frenzy of violently contrasting colours thundering from this painting. Mondrian seemed to be off the track. The once dreamy traditionalist here revealed himself as an iconoclast.

Mill in Sunlight conveys an impression of the moment when the eye tries to focus on a structure that, in the hottest part of day, is blocked from view by the summer sun blazing just behind its pinnacle. The eye is dazzled; blind spots flicker on the retina. The violence of this image, and the *pointille* bring to mind the works of van Gogh, which had recently been shown in Amsterdam. Though Mondrian's palette is limited and crude in comparison to van Gogh's, this work actually tops the older painter's in terms of urgency and excitement.

The foundation for the red, yellow, blue and violet was laid in a wash of thin, gold-ochre, red and blue paint in which Mondrian sketched in broad brushstrokes the big essentials of the image: the sky, the mill and its surroundings. The linear elements of the mill's structure, and especially the use of the palette knife in the shadow and the sky, remind one not so much of van Gogh as of Jan Toorop, who, in the years around the turn of the century, derived his examples from Brussels, Vienna and Switzerland rather than from Paris.[5] In September 1908, a few months before the genesis of *Mill in Sunlight*, Mondrian and Toorop met in the summer light at Walcheren. Mondrian's initial image of international Modernism must certainly have been influenced by their conversations.[6]

For both of them, Luminism was spiritual. This was clearly put into words by Mondrian in 1908 in a letter to Israel Querido, but the letter provoked misunderstanding because of the explicit esoteric connections upon which Mondrian also commented.[7] The spirituality of Luminism was primarily concerned with linking the sensation of light to mood. 'Mood' was an outdated critical term, yet charged with the tension of a new technique, it was capable of catching the genesis of meaning.[8] Jan Sluyters, in a letter from 1910, emphasised not the 'outward distinction of the sifting of colours, not the searching after effect by throwing colours about'. Luminism had to be regarded as the consequence of 'a more violent realisation of the superiority of a mind moved by things above the normal optical awareness.'[9]

Seen in this context, *Mill in Sunlight* is less an impression of a moment than a bearer of everlasting meaning. That there is some truth in this becomes obvious when we take into account the source of *Mill in Sunlight*. The motif of the mill is the direct heir to one of the masterpieces of the Haagse School, *In the Month of July* by Paul Gabriël (fig.6), which Mondrian copied in the Rijksmuseum in 1895.[10] *In the Month of July* is an ode to nature. It depicts a mill in the clear, high sky of a sun-drenched summer's day. On the right, alongside the ditch, a man is walking in the direction of the mill. On the other side is a goat. Neither have influence on the import of what is represented: they belong to the landscape just like the birds and the clouds. The unity of the image is not in the detail, the atmosphere, the colouring. It is space, emphasised by the reflection in the water that almost doubles the presence of the mill, that produces the unity of image as light. The light is all-defining. It arranges space. As distinct from philosophical or religious notions, it represents a spiritual order that transcends the little man and his motives. *In the Month of July* is not a landscape but a 'portrait'. And it is not the portrait of a thing but of a characteristic, a condition that is primarily spiritual. This applies equally to *Mill in Sunlight*, which is also a 'portrait' with all the psychological aspects implied by that term. But unlike Gabriël's, Mondrian's psychological perception is not atmospheric and illusionistic but manifested in the actual characteristics of paint and its very material presence. 'I never painted these things romantically; but from the beginning, I was always a realist', Mondrian said.[11] His *Mill* is a pæon to the unchangeable, timeless quality of the Dutch landscape.

For a certain period Mondrian may well have felt sympathy for questions of the occult; yet we should not forget that as a painter of landscapes he was part of a long Dutch tradition in which such works represented a quest beyond the accidental or temporary to reveal the all-

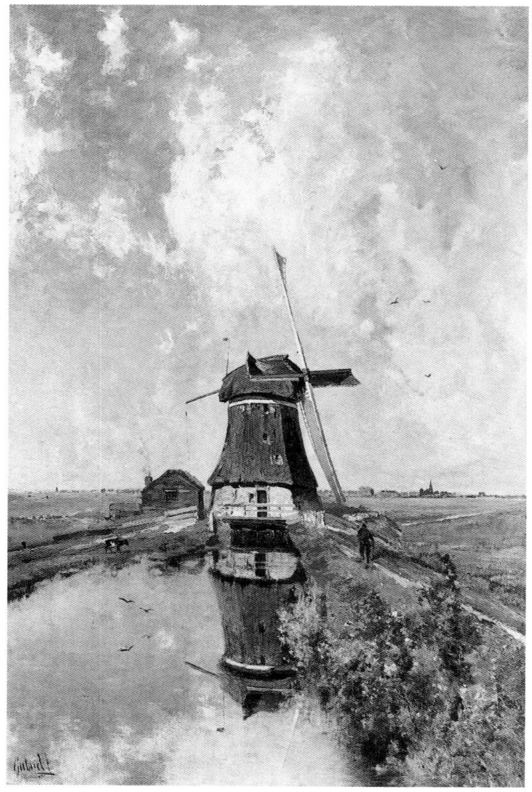

fig.6 PAUL J.C. GABRIËL
In the Month of July: A Windmill on a Polder Waterway
1880, oil on canvas 103 × 66 cm. Rijksmusem Amsterdam

transcending soul of nature. *In the Month of July* is one of many landscapes by Gabriël and others of the Hague School that show a near religious enthusiasm for the Dutch landscape.

According to a longstanding notion, the Dutch *plein air* tradition of the second half of the nineteenth century should be defined exclusively in terms of a tonal Impressionism. The painters of the Hague School adhered to the principle of *alleen maar schilderen* (the Dutch version of art for art's sake) and history has interpreted their works accordingly. Mondrian's early landscapes are placed in this tradition.[12] Robert Welsh in particular has contributed to the propagation of this opinion and in doing so, helped to widen the gap between the perception of the early Mondrian (whose landscapes are part of this tradition) and the Modernistic Mondrian.[13]

Dutch landscape painting of the seventeenth century was, until lately, regarded as an early form of art for art's sake. In recent writings this view has been the subject of a lively discussion with some interesting conclusions – especially Boudewijn Bakker's interpretation of the Dutch landscape as the 'second book' next to the Bible. There is no reason to assume that this tradition did not carry through to the late nineteenth and early twentieth centuries. Even at the beginning of the twentieth century Dutch landscape painting, precisely because of its religious neutrality throughout the centuries, was still connected to the idea of the manifestation of the Divine transcending the temporary and the specific.[14] The expression of the universal may have enticed Mondrian into his Modernistic adventure, but was closely tied to the Dutch landscape tradition.

Red Tree

Like *Mill in Sunlight*, *Red Tree* 1908 (cat.17) is also a 'portrait' – albeit in a different tradition from Gabriël's work. Towards the end of the last century, painters like Willem Witsen and Eduard Karsen applied themselves to painting subdued, introverted nightscapes. Their motifs were presented in frontal isolation, as though seen through a zoom lens, in slowly congealing light and dying colours. In *Red Tree*, the motif of the old fruit tree with its interlocking criss-cross of branches is placed in a sketchy, shallow landscape. The manner of painting distracts attention from the source in both Witsen's and Karsen's work. At the bottom of the image the blue is openly structured and depicted in loose brushstrokes over a thin red and blue wash. The top fans out into short lines that continually change direction, meandering through the surrounding independent deep-blue spots. In the intensely red, linear depiction of the bark, scarlet accents, added late in the painting process, are bundled loosely together. Before this addition the tree was presented as a mass composed of dark blues and blacks. The addition of red changes the status of the light in the painting.

In comparison to *Mill in Sunlight*, *Red Tree*, with its loosely stacked dabs of paint applied in varying degrees of intensity, from scanty and thin to oily and dense, is a tribute to van Gogh.[15] The *pointille* is loose, expressive, follows the motif, and is never given up in favour of another method. The use of colour is highly expressive, the dramatic contrast between the juxtaposed, saturated blue and red lending an extra tension to the tree as a metaphor for autonomous growth and, by implication, the individual. When Mondrian first exhibited the painting in 1910 he called it 'Evening'. Once again he shows his concern with the space of dusk, a space where the 'unweaving of the soul' could take place. The deep blue and fierce red once again add a psychological dimension. Later on, paintings like *Red Mill* 1910–11 (cat.33), in which Mondrian also added the deep red to the lurid blue of the surroundings only in the last stage, were described as 'astral manifestations'.

Light and dark colours

The exact meaning of the light, primary colours of *Mill in Sunlight* and the dark, saturated hues of *Red Tree* would continue to concern Mondrian for a number of years.[16] The opposition seemed to have something to do with the contradiction between inwardness and outwardness, with object and subject, body and mind, between materiality and more subtle areas. But which colour corresponded to which state, and the best policy to adopt remained unclear. For it was certain that the issue was about strategy, about the *a priori* planning of possibilities of meaning in colour. Before embarking on the adventure of Cubism, Mondrian dwelt on the sombre, dense colours, used in big, closed planes as in *Red Mill* and *Evolution* 1910–11 (cat.31). This was probably because he associated the lighter tones with individual exaggeration and easy Impressionism while, as he pointed out later, he linked the intensity of saturated colours to calmness, immutability, pureness and the inner self.[17]

In Paris, when Mondrian sought to learn from Picasso's palette, his objective was the invariable expression of the universal. In *Composition III in Colour* 1913 (cat.48) for instance, Mondrian based his use of colour, mainly ochres and greys, on Picasso's example. That this was a practical alternative for the representation of the timeless, near-religious content for which Mondrian was searching may be demonstrated by Theo van Doesburg's review, written after he had made his first acquaintance with Mondrian's work in 1916. With his greys, white and ochres, Picasso reached a 'metaphysical palette' and, according to van Doesburg, 'reduced the prismatic colouring of the luminists to white, black, grey and sepia'. Speaking from experience van Doesburg sees the black, white and grey used by Mondrian as befitting works of a 'purely spiritual content. The feeling that came over me when seeing [*Composition 10 in Black and White: Pier and Ocean* 1915; fig.1] was immaculately spiritual; almost religious, be it less enthusiastic. Yet it doesn't lack the power which the nature painters of the nineteenth century concentrated on their canvases to express sunlight. It might even have been inspired by sunlight.'[18]

For his first Cubist works Mondrian rejected the strategy of the dark, saturated colours, limiting himself to light reds, yellows and blues, but used with such subtlety that their intensity is hardly perceptible. In *The Sea* 1912 (cat.36) the primary colours are scarcely effective, but in *Flowering Appletree* (cat.38), painted the same year, they enliven the grey and respond to the weaving of lines. Line and colour here do not model objects; they exclusively model their mutual relationships. *Composition 6* (cat.49) of two years later shows the blue, the ochre and the soft pink as gradations of the blue-grey background. The result emanates light and atmosphere. This was exactly what annoyed van Doesburg. In a letter to the poet Anthonie Kok he wrote in 1917: 'The painters of the past tried to express their emotion by way of tone. Music had already done this. That's why the term "tone" is borrowed from music, with regard to painting, breaking of colours. Regarding music tone is: breaking of sound. In painting this has led to painting with dirt. This used to be called sentiment art.'[19] That this matter had already played a part in their earlier discussions is shown by a letter that Mondrian wrote to van Doesburg two years earlier in which he warns against dogmatism and the urge to adopt an absolute position. He insisted on the need for relativity and subtlety in the matter of choice, gradation and saturation of colour. 'I am not abandoning colour, but I want it just as intense as possible.'[20]

In texts written in those years and later to be published as 'De Nieuwe Beelding in de Schilderkunst' (The New Plastic in Painting), Mondrian enters into a discussion of the role of colour.[21] He makes a distinction between natural and primary colour. Natural colour, used by generations of artists to depict reality, invests the object with an outward appearance through the light cast upon it. Primary colour is completely different: it is distinguished by an interiorising quality, for which, he claimed, the world was not yet ready. Until that time, painting that used it would have to 'rely upon the primary colours, supplemented by white, black and grey.' And he adds in a note: 'Grey, too, because just as yellow, blue and red it can be mixed with white and remain *basic colour*, so can black.'[22]

Here we have an explanation for why Mondrian mixed red, yellow and blue with white in the Cubist work: because of the difference between theory and practice. 'I use those subdued colours temporarily, adjusting myself to the present environment and world; it does not prevent me from preferring pure colour. Otherwise you might think I contradicted myself in my work.'[23] Moreover, the primary colours are chosen in such a way that their relationship on the canvas is overtly interdependent. This should not, he said, be disturbed by the personal input of the artist: 'the principle thing is that *colour be free of individuality and individual sensations and that it expresses only the serene emotion of the universal*.' In a note he elaborates: 'That is, they will not imitate astral colour, for example.'[24] Neither the independent qualities of the colour nor the qualities assigned to it by the artist play a role in the painting Mondrian had in view.

With his remark about astral colours, Mondrian seems to distance himself from the saturated hues of *Red Tree*, *Red Mill* and *Evolution*. But it is not that clear-cut. Earlier in the text he had labelled yellow and blue as 'most inward' while he described red as 'most outward', an opinion he maintained until around 1929.[25] If colour represents meaning and expression it has to be a universal, general meaning formulated in every separate colour and specified in the relational unity of the image. Unity and relationship are the determinants in the origination of meaning in colour. Yet, perhaps not wishing to burn his boats, he offers no opinion on the question of whether colour carries an inner meaning of its own. His need to make the universal visible forces him to keep available the possibilities of the pure, saturated colour as used in *Red Mill*. The visualisation of intense spiritual life in his view requires flat and saturated colours. Conventionality of colour is not excluded in the New Plastic: above all it is the effect that counts. In additional essays written after the first installments of 'The New Plastic in Painting' appeared in *De Stijl*, Mondrian specifies the intended effect of the image: 'Unity, in its most profound essence, *radiates*; it *is*. The radiation of unity's *being* wrecks itself upon the physical ... The *ray* is the symbol of radiation (the inward).'[26] Unity is not only dictated by the visual means of line, colour and composition. Much more important is the radiation emanating from the image itself, making visible the inner self. Mondrian is speaking here of the soft, unceasing radiation of the image that in *Red Tree* was responsible for the 'unweaving of the soul'.

After 1914 Mondrian's compositions are usually constructed from a centre. *Composition 6* (cat.49) radiates from the centre but is fixed by the edges of the canvas. The outward movement supports the colour, which strives after the realisation of a clear, radiating power. The majority of *pentimenti* in the paintings of this period are to be found in the upper middle part of the picture plane, where the light originates. Often, there are many layers of paint, and white usually turns out to be Mondrian's solution, introducing a strange materiality in the image and emphasising the light in a physical way. It is not an atmospheric, illusory light, but a soft glow carried by the surface.

Mondrian chooses toned-down colours because he believes that clarity and power can be achieved in a quiet, considered way. But he also seems to hesitate, as if he does not know how to invest his spiritualised colour with the optimum effect. In *Composition in Oval with Colour Planes 2* 1914 (cat.50) for instance, he loosens the reins again, mixing less white through the colours and trying out a higher degree of saturation. Along with their subtlety the colour fields lose their materiality and physicality. They now behave like the samples in a colour fan, no longer referring to equivalents in reality but to a specific, independent texture. The qualities of each colour slowly emerge. The thin, receding strips that Mondrian used as frames from 1914 onwards push the image forward and accentuate its presence in terms of the reflection of light.

Chequerboards

In 1919 Mondrian made two paintings based on a completely regular, geometric grid. In *Composition Chequerboard: Light Colours* 1919 (cat.59), the grid of sixteen horizontal and sixteen vertical rectangular planes is filled with salmon pink, bright yellow, soft blue, dark grey, light grey and white. There is no repetition, or uniformity, but neither is there arbitrariness or chaos. Equilibrium is lent a helping hand by the system of thin black lines, and in some places light grey lines, separating the planes.

In the somewhat smaller *Composition Chequerboard: Dark Colours* 1919 (cat.58), Mondrian uses no white or grey, only a deep saturated blue, a fierce deep pink and a dark yellow ochre separated by a system of grey and, here and there, greenish lines. The smaller format and the absence of the white and the greys create a much more concentrated and dense effect than that of its peer, which is bright and airy in tone. The way in which the paint is applied also differs in each of these two works. The light chequerboard is loosely painted in thin, mostly flat paint with a luminous, almost atmospheric result, while the dark chequerboard is much oilier, thicker and more material. The saturated glowing colours that Mondrian

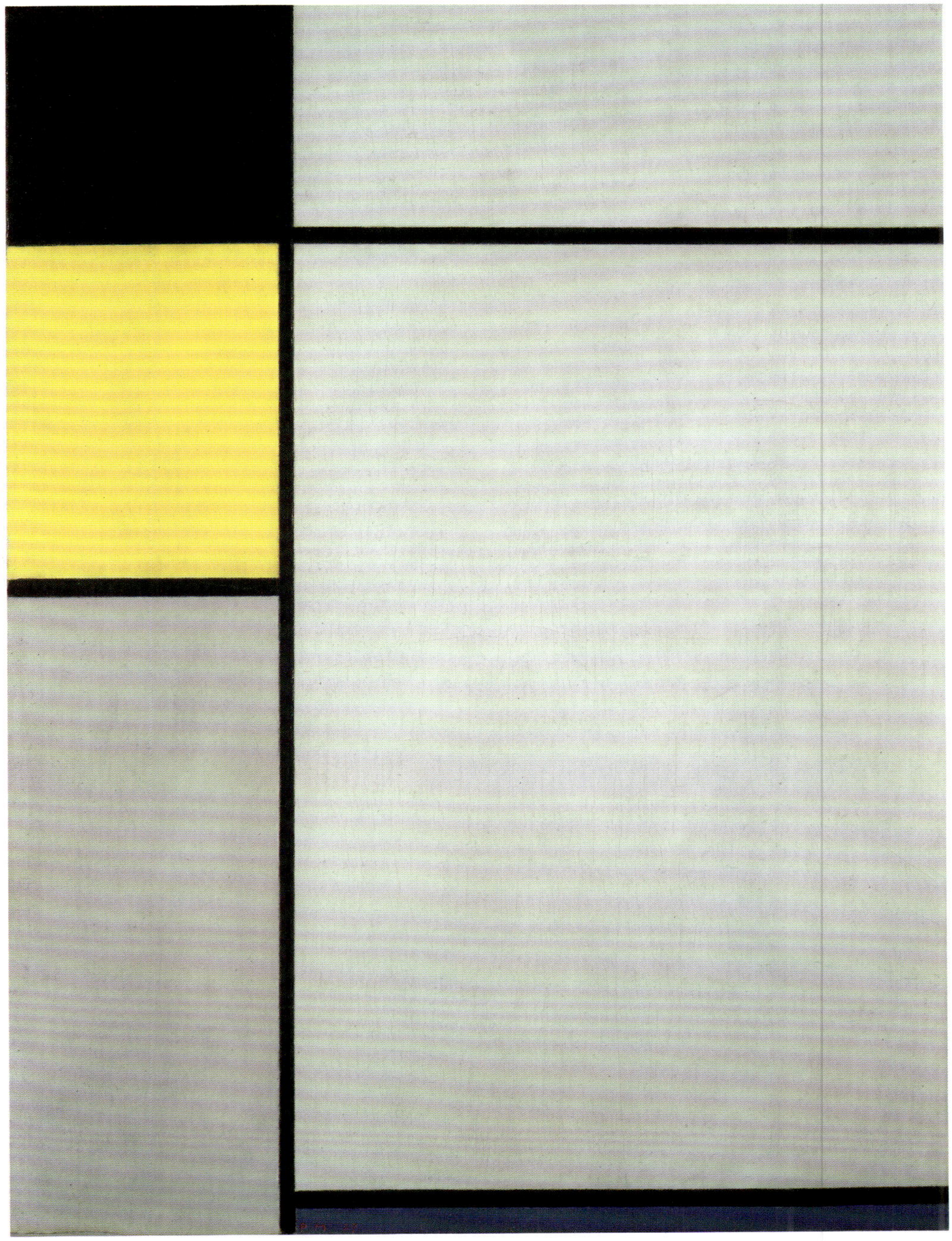

fig.7

Composition No.1: Composition with Black, Yellow and Blue

1927, oil on canvas 73 × 54 cm. Private Collection,
courtesy Annely Juda Fine Art, London

employed so often in his earlier works are applied here largely by palette knife. Neither painting, however, achieves the clarity of the later Neo-plastic works where the visual elements are much more tightly defined and handled.

In the two chequerboard compositions Mondrian is seemingly attempting to decide once and for all on a colour strategy for Neo-plasticism. On his return from Holland to Paris on 21 June 1919, he appears to have opted for that of *Composition Chequerboard: Light Colours*: the majority of the works he produced in Paris from 1920 onwards are characterised by gradations of red, yellow and blue with white, grey and dark or bluish grey. Yet well into the 1920s the colour strategy of *Composition Chequerboard: Dark Colours* also remains operative. An example is *Composition No.1: Composition with Black, Yellow and Blue* of 1927 (fig.7). This marvellous painting is dominated by a shimmering, deep yellow plane, which, flanked by a matt black plane and a thin strip of dark blue at the bottom of the picture, keeps in check three dark grey areas. The colour fields are situated along the edges, but are not able to break through the density of the dark grey planes. Framing the painting is a thin strip of wood, the dark colour of which has an important encompassing effect. The brushstrokes also sustain the closed structure; although explicitly present, they are soft and subdued. The grey of the elongated horizontal and vertical planes is painted crosswise in both directions while the big grey area and the yellow portion are painted vertically, which has the effect that the large grey area looks lighter than the elongated areas. The blue strip and the black plane are flat and painted in a horizontal direction, and the black lines separating the planes are very shiny, lacking any texture whatsoever. They constitute the only static moment in an image that is otherwise, paradoxical as it may seem, generously infused with movement. Light is reflected in many different ways by the various textures, assisting visual clarity and contrast. The planes act like the facets of a diamond, always suggesting different directions and continually drawing attention to other sides of the object.

Yellow Lines

Towards the end of the 1920s Mondrian reduced the number of colours to two, later even to one. At the same time the shades in the white planes became closer to each other. Finally, in 1930, Mondrian chose the same saturated mixture for all the white planes. Only the variation in the direction of the brushstrokes causes a dissimilarity between the single planes, breaking the light differently on every plane and giving the illusion of another, continually varying colour. Around 1932 the black line still separating the planes divided into two. At that moment Mondrian wrote enthusiastically to an old friend: 'I am doing new research: canvases with double lines through which I achieve a greater clarity.'[27] In a number of other paintings Mondrian also omitted all use of colour so that the image could be dominated completely by an imposing, shiny black system of lines, sometimes only differing in width.

The contrast between the shiny black and the clear, saturated white, increased to a maximum, resulted in some glorious works.

Around this time Mondrian wrote an enigmatic text under the title *L'Art Réaliste et l'art Superréaliste*, published in 1931 in a Dutch volume along with contributions by mostly Dutch artists.[28] Describing once more the basic assumptions of his work, he emphasises that modern art has no dogmas, that every artist and his group must pursue their own ideas about beauty, and that there are no ubiquitous laws that can bring about universal beauty. Indisputable to Mondrian, however, is the evolution of art towards the positive and the good. Then follows a strange passage in which he elaborates on the opposition between nightfall and daybreak. He sets the tragic against the light, suffering against life, darkness against hope, fear against future, death against evolution and despair against optimism. Dusk and dawn are the moments of transition on which he concentrates. Almost ecstatically he goes on to proclaim that mankind has arrived at the stage of dawn. And he proceeds: 'This is how we must understand the great classic art of the past: as works created in the harmonious light of the full moon. Their creation was not possible in full daylight. If such work can still be produced today, at dawn, it is because of night's reflection and because the conception of full daylight is not yet clear. But just as artificial light increasingly conquers night, the man of complete daylight will conquer night ... Let us now live in full daylight, so that we can create ... Let us paint the idea of the bright full day.'[29]

This text marks the moment when Mondrian once and for all broke all ties with the Symbolist legacy, the ties which had kept him a prisoner of the opposition between the subjective and the objective for so long and had determined his work well into the 1920s. Within this context, in 1932–3, Mondrian started *Composition with Yellow Lines* (cat.64), whose contrasting white and yellow creates a clarity that scintillates with the same qualities as a clear sparkling sky in the early morning. After a career of almost fifty years, in *Composition with Yellow Lines* Mondrian finally brought about the light that had concerned him as a painter throughout his entire life.

NOTES

1 See C. Blotkamp, *Destruction as Art*, London 1994, p.211 and Yve-Alain Bois, 'The Iconoclast' in *Piet Mondrian: 1872–1944*, exh. cat., National Gallery of Washington and the Museum of Modern Art, New York 1994, p.357.

2 Piet Mondrian, 'Towards the True Vision of Reality', as cited in: Harry Holtzmann and Martin James (ed.), *The New Art – The New Life: The Collected Writings of Piet Mondrian*, London 1987, p.338.

3 Bois 1994, p.313.

4 Israel Querido, '(Van Menschen en Dingen.) Een schildersstudie. Spoor, Sluyters, Piet Mondriaan', *De Controleur*, vol.19, 29 May 1909, pp.1–3.

5 In the second half of the 1880s Jan Toorop used the palette-knife extensively, instructed by Vogels and Ensor. A good example is *The Sea*, which Toorop painted in 1887 (Rijksmuseum Amsterdam). For the idea that the reception of Neo-Impressionism in the Nether-

lands came about mainly through Jan Toorop, cf. Gertrud Wendermann, *Studien zur Rezeption des Neo-Impressionismus in den Niederlanden*, Münster/Hamburg 1993. After 1900, Toorop's contacts with Austria and Switzerland were much stronger than those with Brussels, and should not be underestimated (see n.6).

6 It would be worthwhile to research this relationship more thoroughly. The odd white wooden frames that Mondrian used for *Mill* and other paintings, and his use of the monogram during these years have connections with Giovanni Giacometti, cf. *Giovanni Giacometti, 1868–1933*, exh. cat., Winterthur Kunstmuseum 1996. An understanding of Mondrian's relationship with Swiss traditions may also shed light on the specific way in which he technically assimilated Luminism.

7 Blotkamp 1994, pp.35, 42, 64.

8 For the importance of the terminology invented by the Beweging van Tachtig to the critical reception of the innovations in modern Dutch art around 1905–7 see Fredric Baas, *Vroeger was het gras groener. Negentiende-eeuwse invloeden in de kunstkritiek van begin deze eeuw*, Groningen 1997 (paper delivered in the seminar on The Critical Reception of Early Abstract Painting in Holland Between 1904–1914, written under the supervision of Dr Peter de Ruiter of the Rijksuniversiteit Groningen and the author in autumn 1996).

9 L. van Ginneken and J.M. Joosten, 'Documentatie': kunstenaarsbrieven Kees Spoor, *Museumjournaal*, vol.15, 1970, p.263.

10 See Ronald de Leeuw, John Sillevis, Charles Dumas (eds.), *Haagse School, Hollandse Meesters van de 19e eeuw*, exh. cat., Haags Gemeentemuseum, The Hague 1983, p.183.

11 Op. cit. n.2.

12 For the importance of the notion of 'stemming' (mood) in the art criticism of the 1880s, see Carel Blotkamp, 'The Art Criticism in De Nieuwe Gids', *Simiolus*, vol.5, no.1/2, 1971, pp.113–36 and, more recently, Baas 1997.

13 Robert P. Welsh, *Piet Mondrian's Early Career: The 'Naturalistic' Periods*, New York and London 1965; and also *The Hague School: Dutch Masters of the Nineteenth Century*, Royal Academy, London, and Haags Gemeentemuseum, The Hague 1983.

14 Boudewijn Bakker, 'Levenspelgrimage of vrome wandeling? Claes Jansz. Visscher en zijn serie *Plaisante Plaetsen*', *Oud Holland*, no.107, 1993, pp.97–115, and Huigen Leeflang, 'Het landschap in boek en prent. Perceptie en interpretatie van vroeg zeventiende eeuwse Nederlandse landschapsprenten' in Boudewijn Bakker en Huigen Leeflang, *Nederland naar 't leven: Landschapsprenten uit de Gouden Eeuw*, exh. cat., Museum Het Rembrandthuis, Amsterdam, and Zwolle 1994, pp.18–32.

15 *Mill in Sunlight* and *Red Tree* have broad, white wooden frames which, almost unsmoothed, probably originally showed the rough grain of the wood (see Frits Lapidoth, 'Kunst in de Hoofdstad III. Het Stedelijk Museum', *De Nieuwe Courant*, 23 Jan. 1909). With these frames Mondrian showed his preference for displaying his works in the manner of the circle around van Gogh *c.*1900. Although originating in lack of money, the method provided the paintings with a certain natural simplicity facilitating the expression of the spiritual. Regarding van Gogh's frames see Louis van Tilborgh, 'Framing Van Gogh 1880–1990', in *In Perfect Harmony: Picture and Frame 1850–1920*, exh. cat., Van Gogh Museum, Amsterdam 1995, pp.163–80 and especially pp.172–6. See n.6.

16 J.M. Joosten, 'Painting and Sculpture in the Context of De Stijl', in *De Stijl 1917–1931: Visions of Utopia*, exh. cat., Walker Art Center, Minneapolis, Hirschhorn Museum and Sculpture Garden, Smithsonian Insitution, Washington, Stedelijk Museum, Amsterdam, and Rijksmuseum Kröller-Müller, Otterlo 1982, pp.114–19.

17 Letter to Augusta de Meester-Obreen of August 1915, partly published in *Elsevier's Geïllustreerd Maandschrift* and published by Wim van Dam, 'Een onbekende brief van Piet Mondriaan', *Oud Holland*, no.104, 1990, pp.341–3. It is remarkable that most of the comments Mondrian made on the subject of colour, and its relationship with expressed emotion are to be found in this letter. Some of them were first published by James Johnson Sweeney in 'Piet Mondrian', *The Museum of Modern Art Bulletin*, vol.12, no.4, Spring 1945.

18 Theo van Doesburg, 'Kunstkritiek', *De Eenheid* no.6, 11 Nov. 1915.

19 Letter from van Doesburg to Anthonie Kok of 3 May 1917, van Doesburg Archives, Rijksbureau voor Kunsthistorische Documentatie, The Hague.

20 Letter to van Doesburg, 20 November 1915, as quoted by Sweeney 1945.

21 Piet Mondrian, 'De Nieuwe Beelding in de Schilderkunst', *De Stijl*, vol.1, no.3, June 1918, p.23, published in English as 'The New Plastic in Painting. Part 3. The New Plastic as Abstract-Real Painting: Plastic Means and Composition', in Holtzmann and James 1987, pp.35–40.

22 ibid., p.36 note d.

23 Letter to van Doesburg of 13 February 1919, van Doesburg Archives, Rijksbureau voor Kunsthistorische Documentatie, The Hague.

24 op cit. n.21, p.36.

25 In a letter to Alfred Roth of 7 September 1929, in response to a request to buy a painting, Mondrian asked him 'si vous préférez bleu et jaune, blanc et gris, ou bien rouge, peu de bleu et de jaune. Ces dernières oeuvres (avec du rouge) sont plus 'reèl', les autres plus spirituel[les] plus ou moins.' Cf. Serge Lemoine (ed.), *Piet Mondrian/Alfred Roth Correspondances*, Paris 1994, p.37.

26 op. cit. n.21, p.48 note j.

27 Letter from Piet Mondrian to the architect, Oud, of 22 December 1932, Institut Néerlandais, Paris.

28 Piet Mondrian, *L'Art réaliste et l'art superréaliste (La morphoplastique et la Néo-plastique)*, in Holtzmann and James 1987, pp.22–35. The text, written for *Cercle et Carré*, was only published in part. It was also partly published in Paul Citroen (ed.), *Palet*, Amsterdam 1931, pp.76–82, which indicates that Mondrian wanted to keep the Dutch public up to date on his current thoughts on the subject.

29 Holtzmann and James 1987, p.229.

COLOUR PLATES

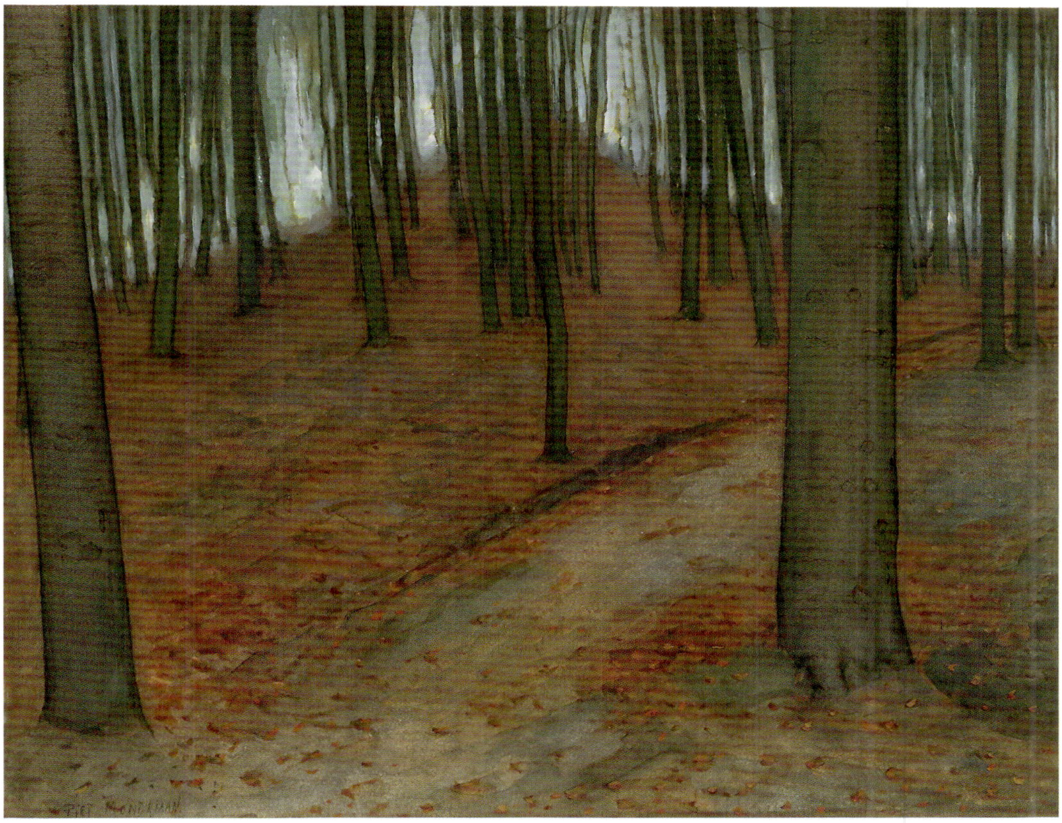

Forest

1898–1900 45.5 × 57cm [cat.1]

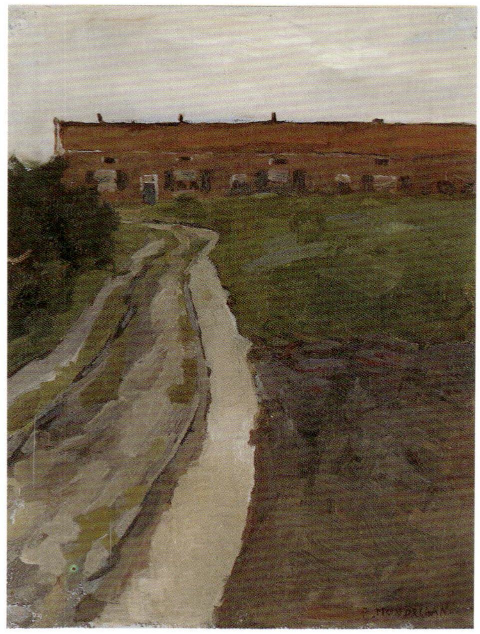

Country Road and Row of Houses

?c.1898 39 × 29.5cm [cat.2]

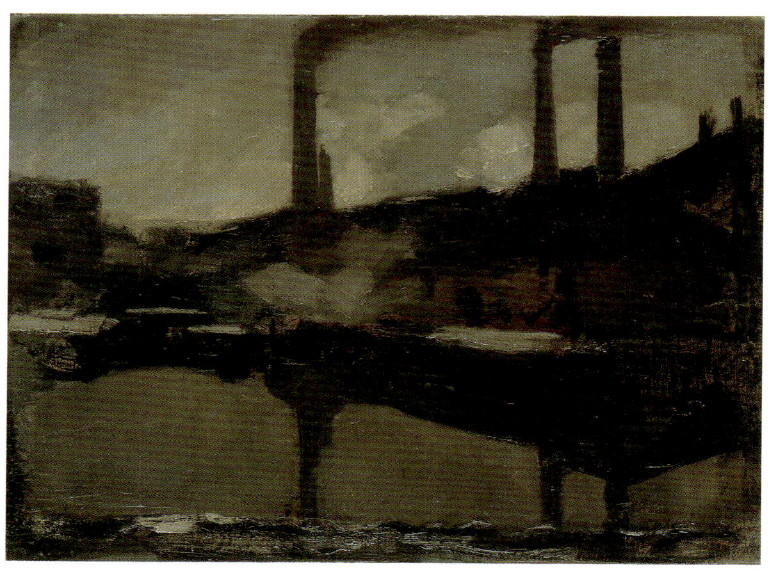

Wax Candle Factory

1900–1 35 × 48cm [cat.3]

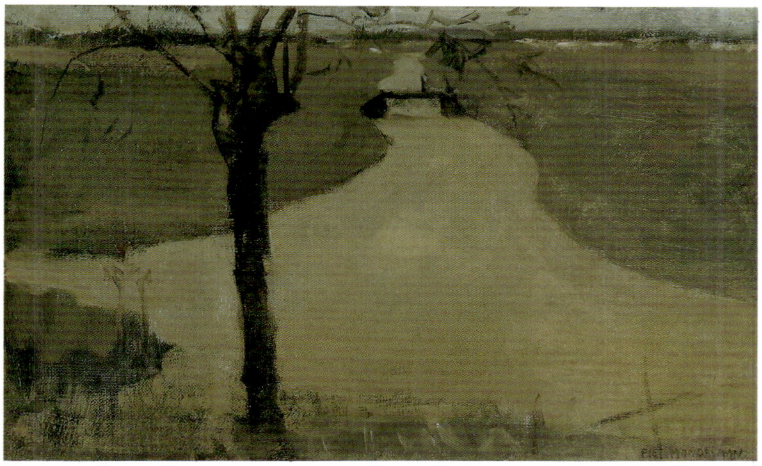

Ditch near the Gein

1901–2 23.5 × 37.5cm [cat.4]

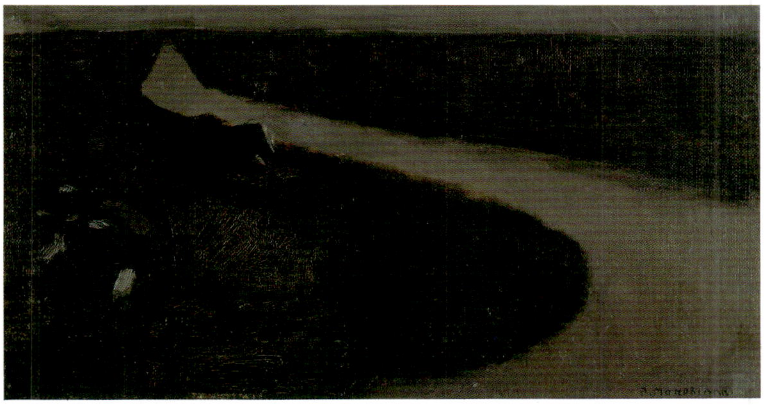

Ditch and Cows

1901–2 20.5 × 38.5cm [cat.5]

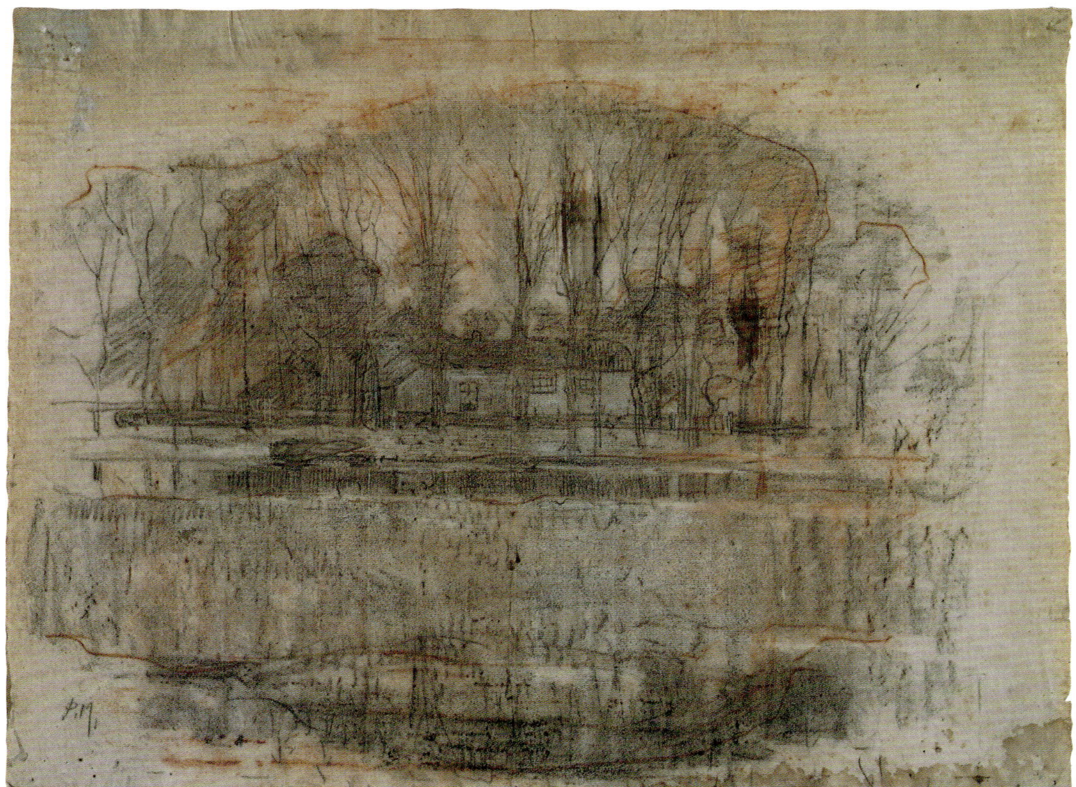

Farm with Trees and Water

1906 47.5 × 61.5cm [cat.6]

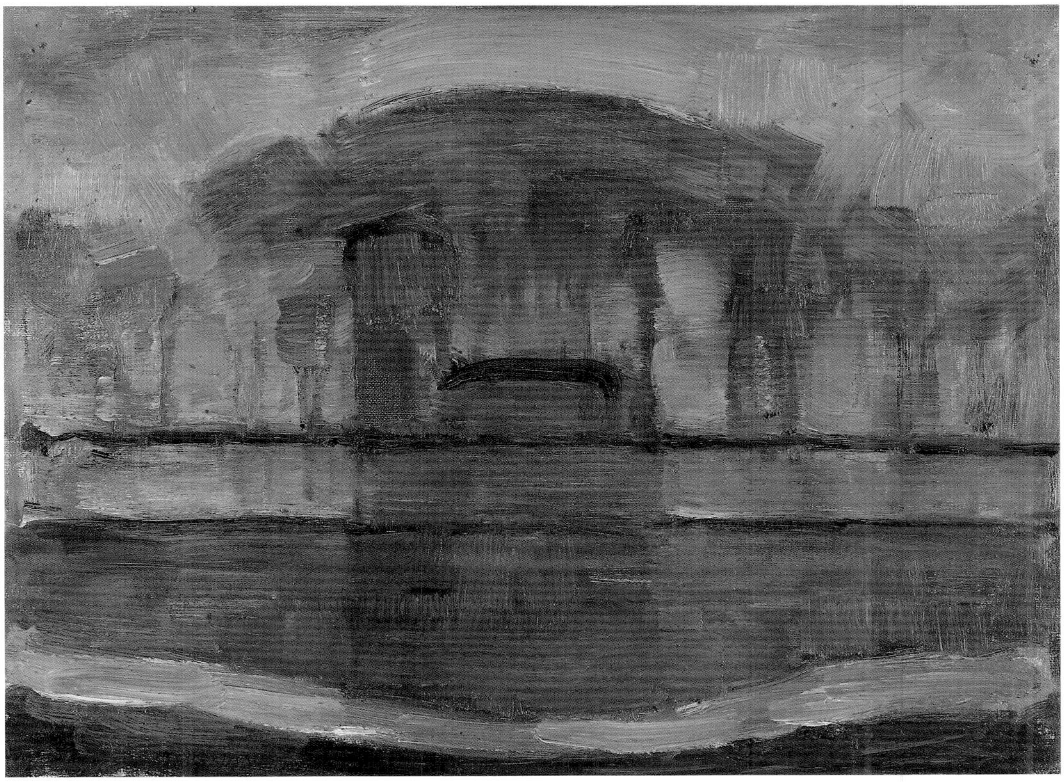

Geinrust Farm in the Mist

1906–7 32.5 × 42.5cm [cat.7]

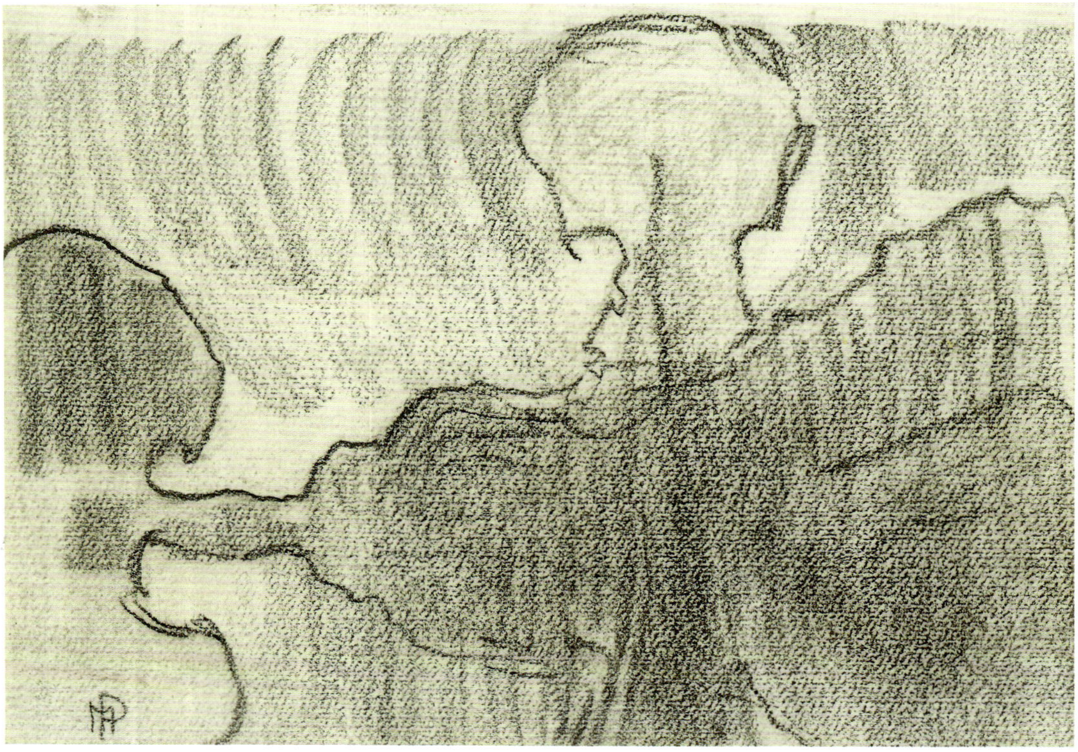

Solitary Tree

?1907 14 × 19cm [cat.8]

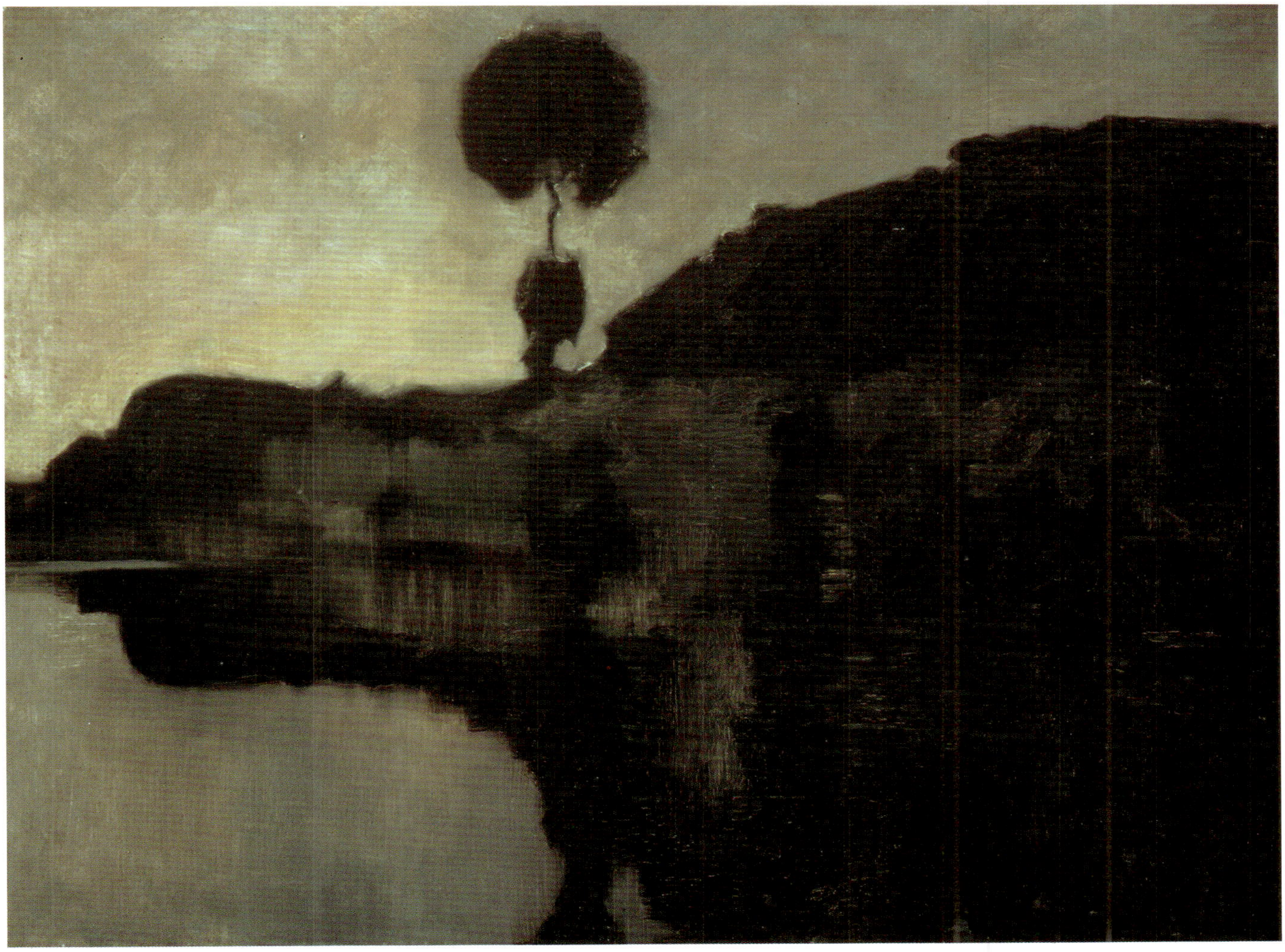

Evening on the Gein

1906 65 × 86cm [cat.9]

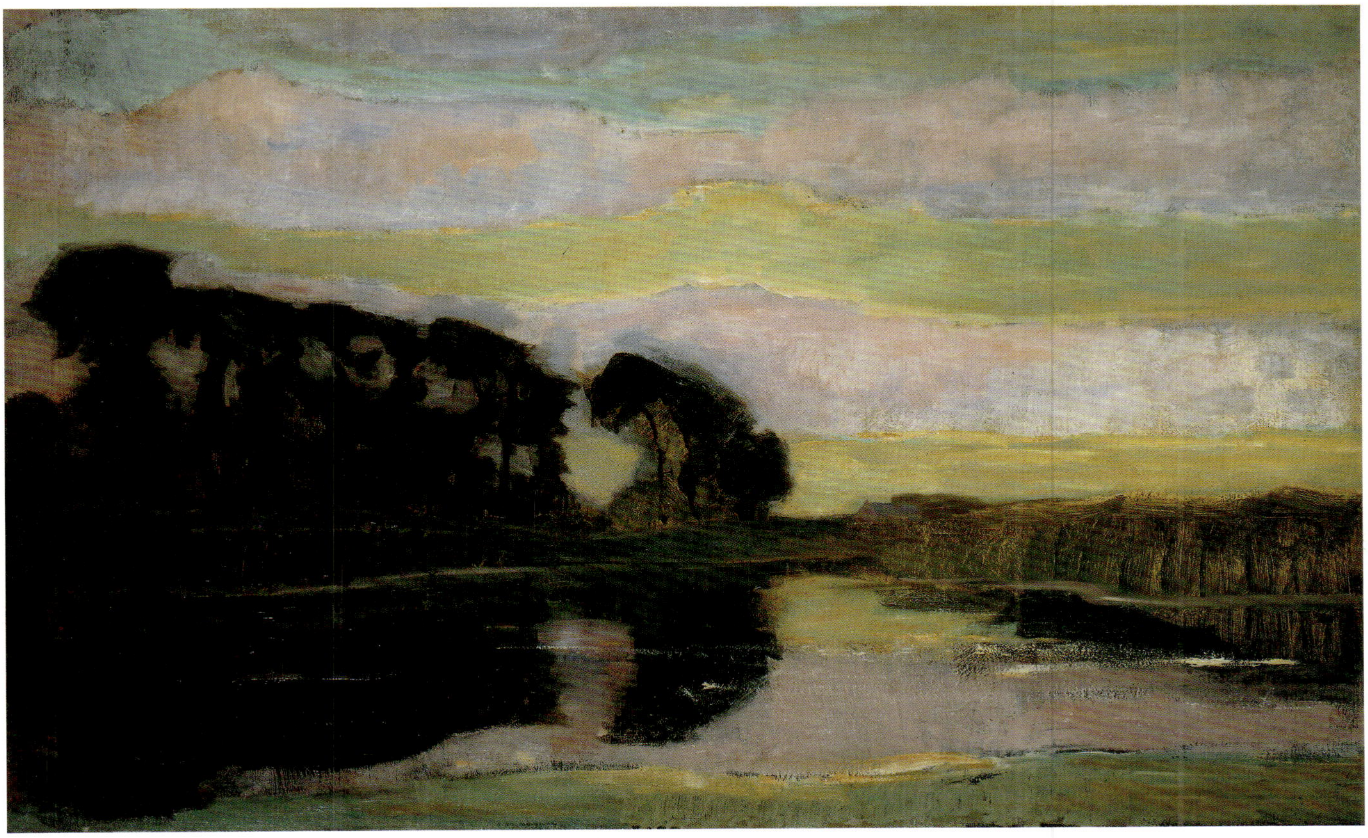

Large Landscape

1907 75 × 120cm [cat.10]

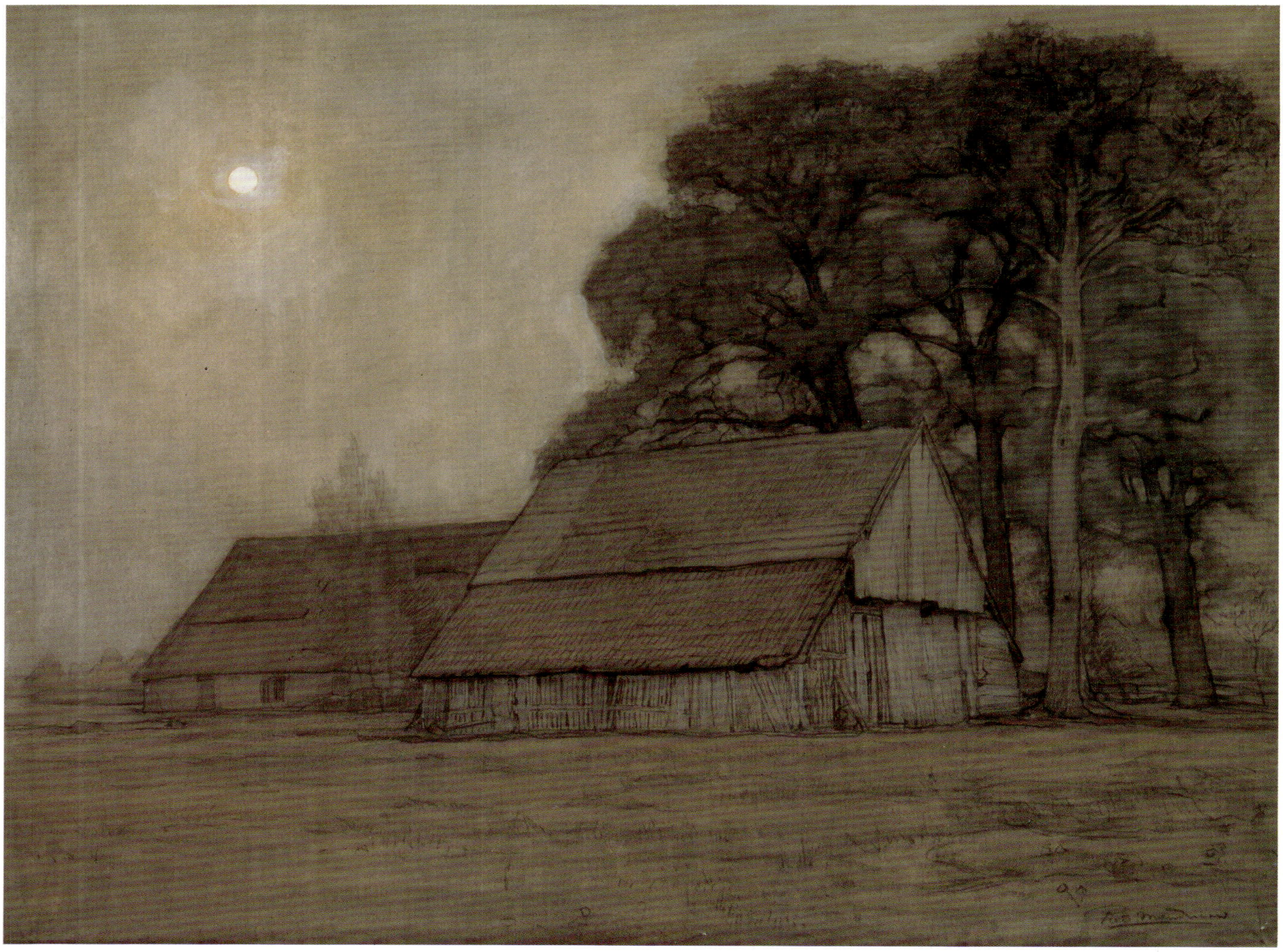

Sheepfold in the Evening

1906 74 × 98cm [cat.11]

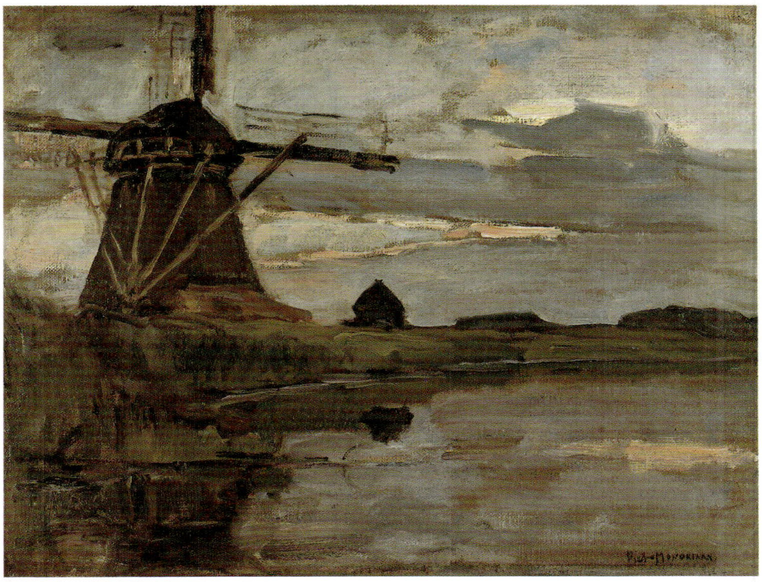

Mill on the Gein

1906–7 34.5 × 44.5cm [cat.12]

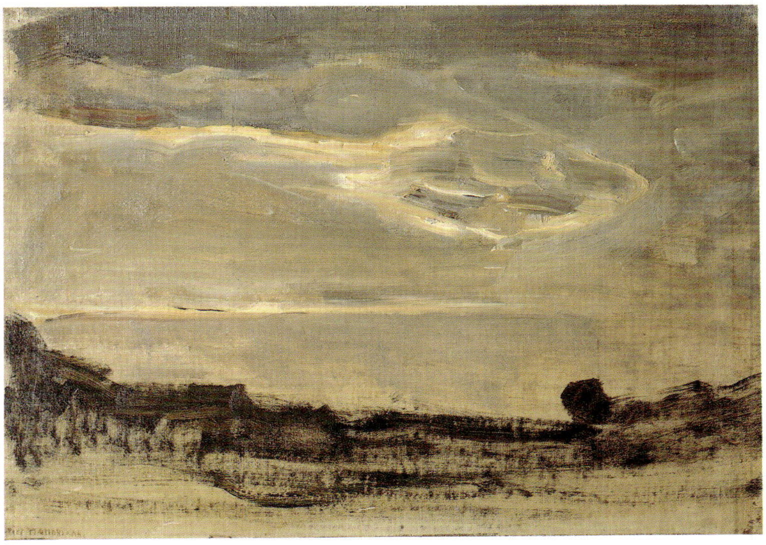

Landscape with Cloud

1907 36 × 49.5cm [cat.13]

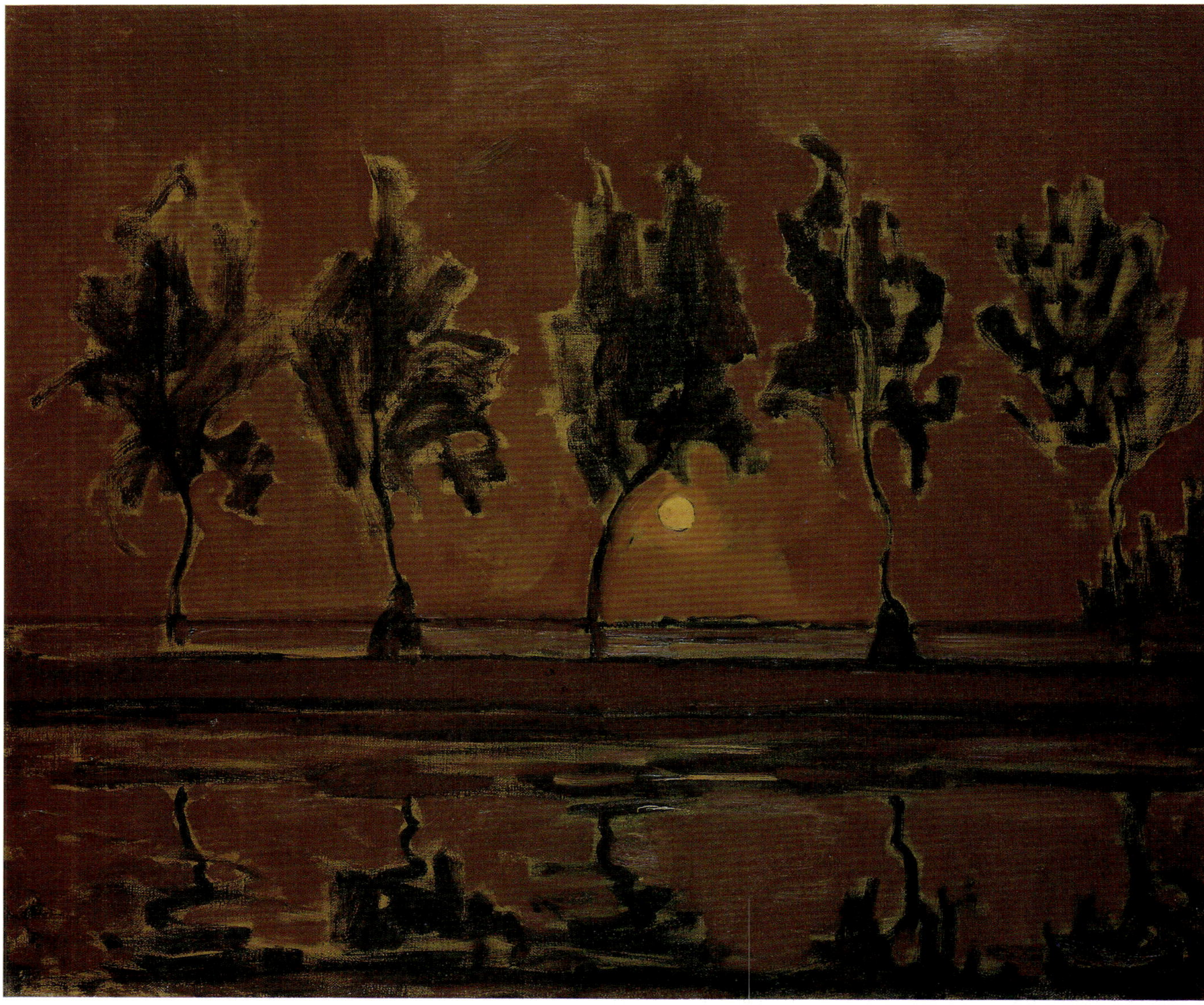

Trees on the Gein: Moonrise

1907–8 79 × 92.5cm [cat.14]

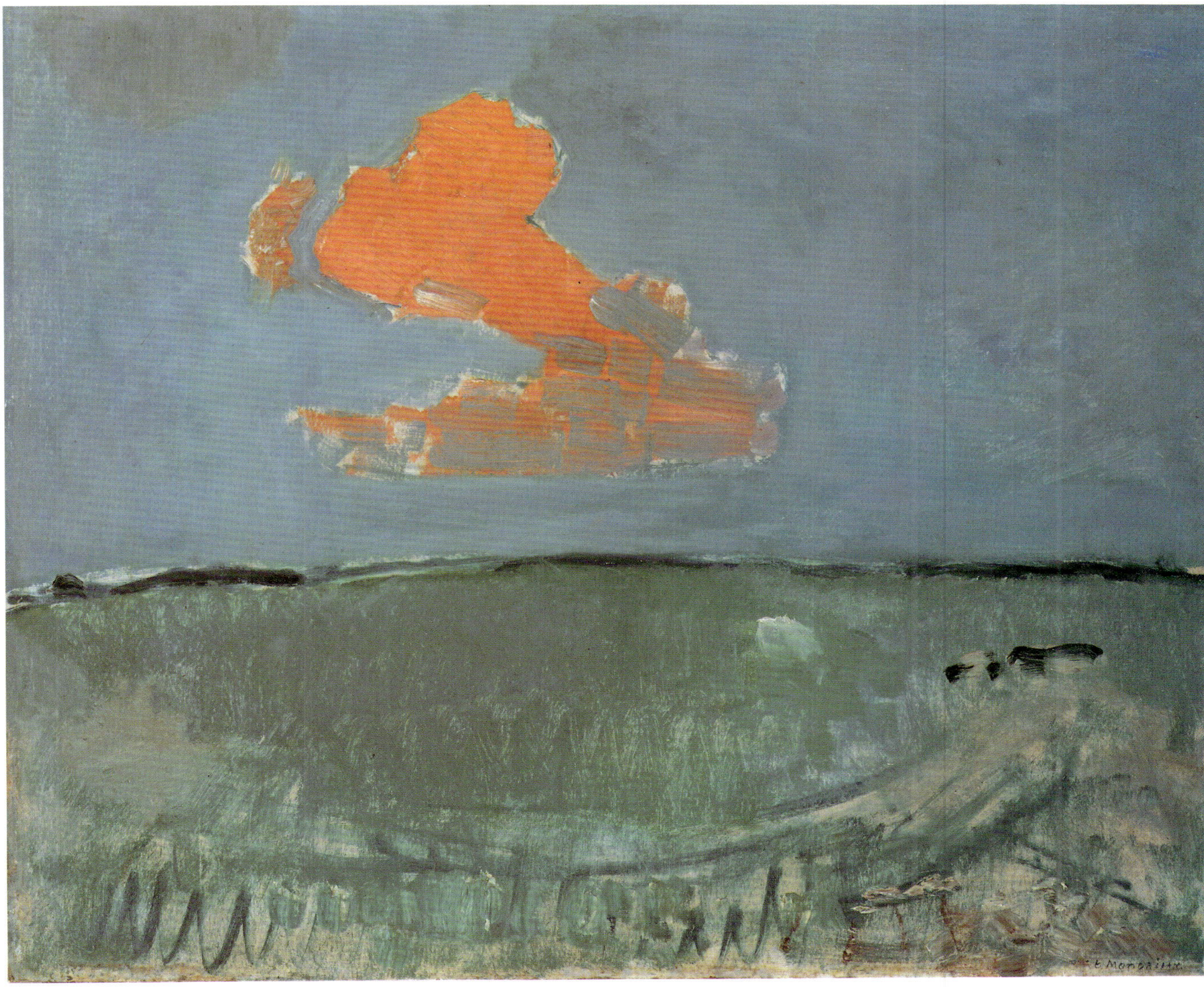

Red Cloud

1907 64 × 75cm [cat.15]

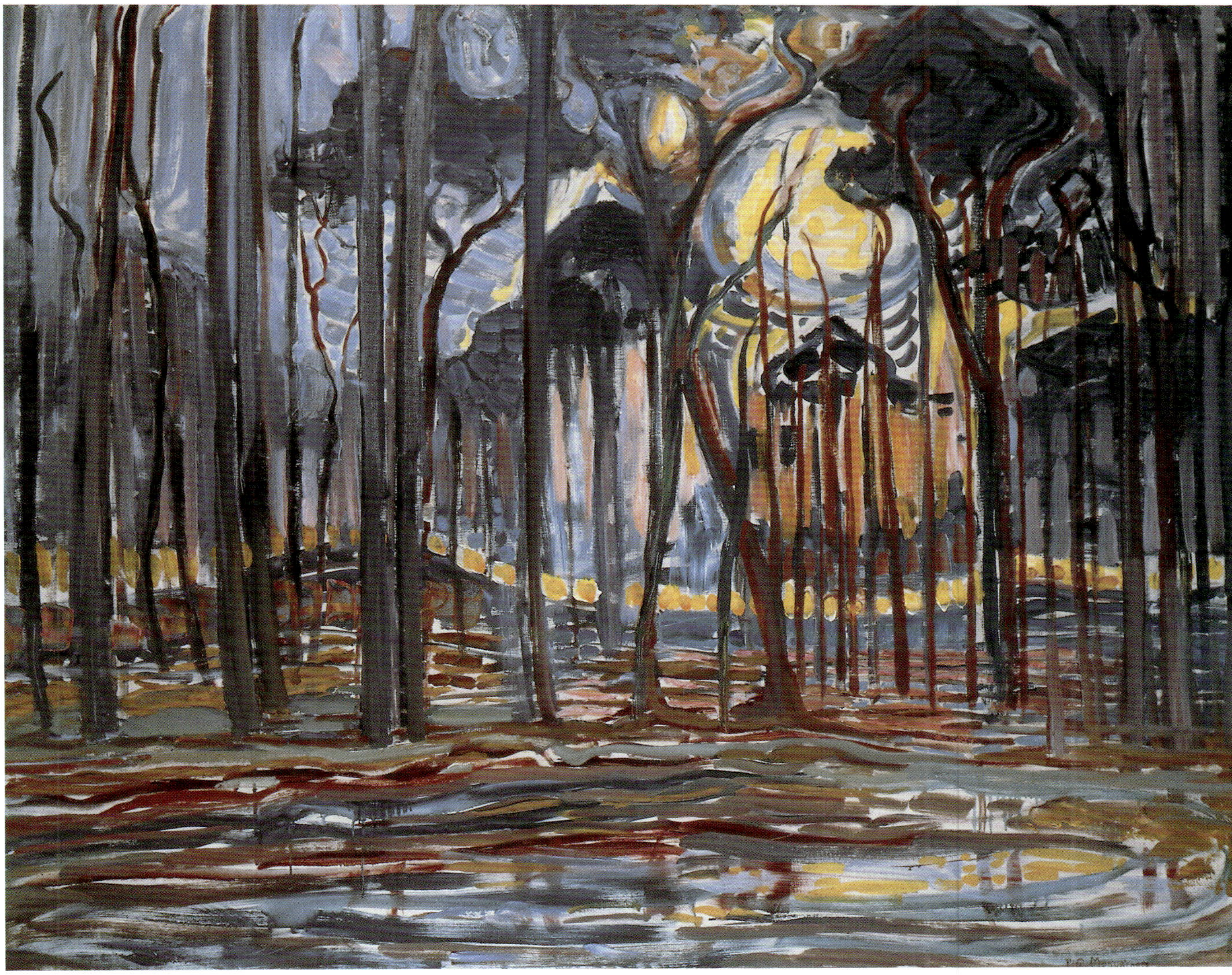

Woods near Oele

1908 128 × 158cm [cat.16]

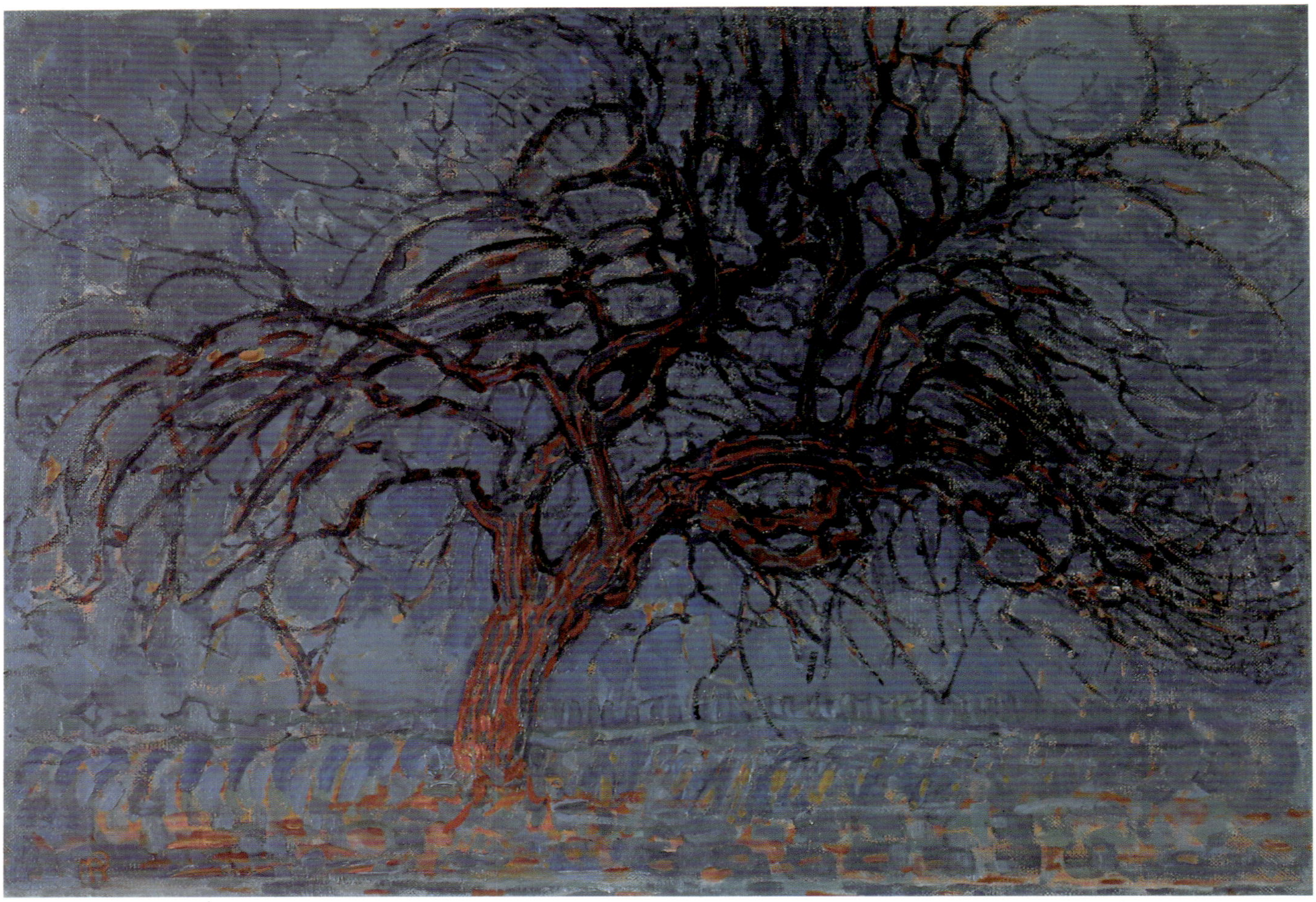

Red Tree

1908 70 × 99cm [cat.17]

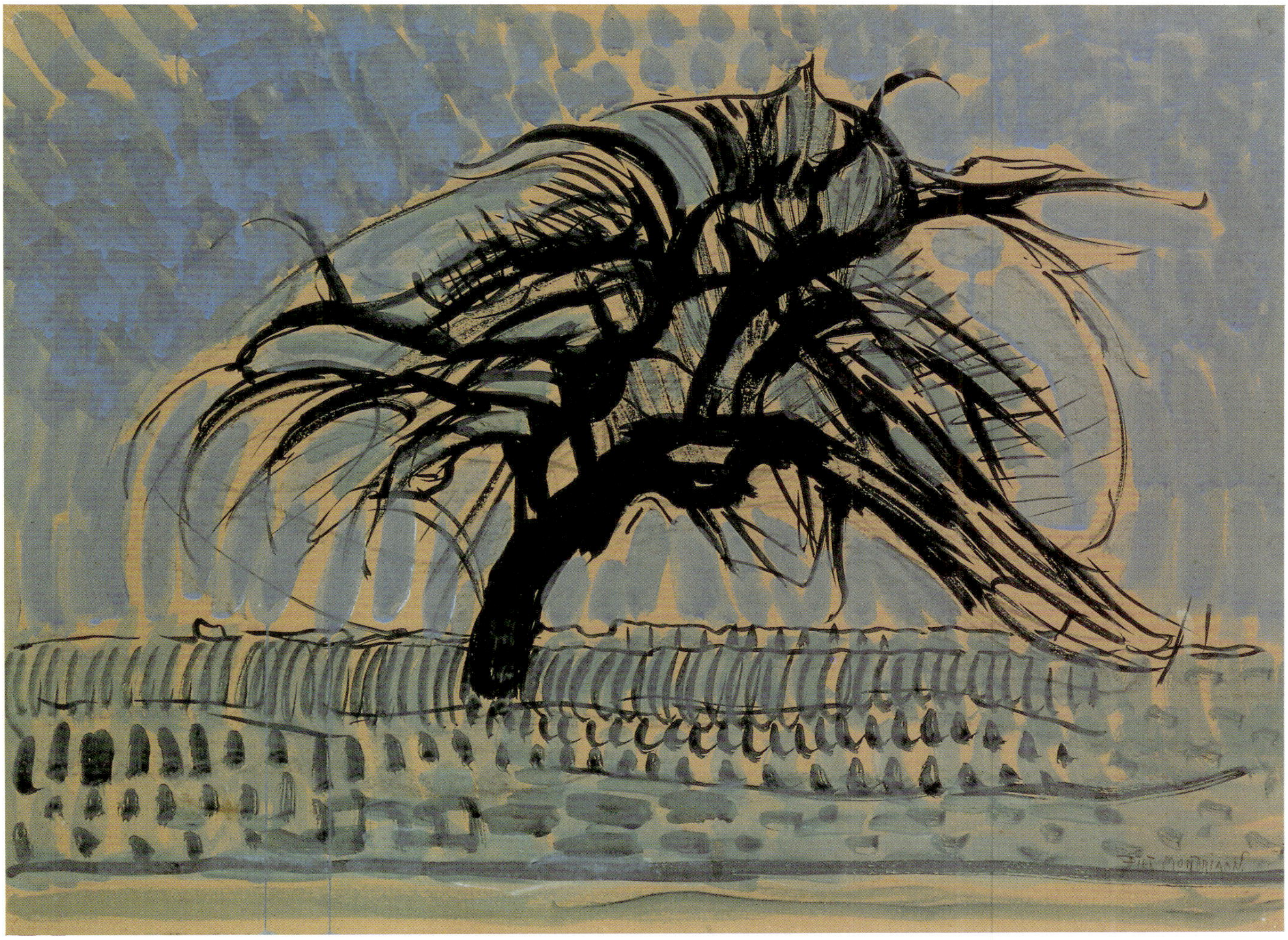

Blue Tree

1908–9 75.5 × 99.5cm [cat.18]

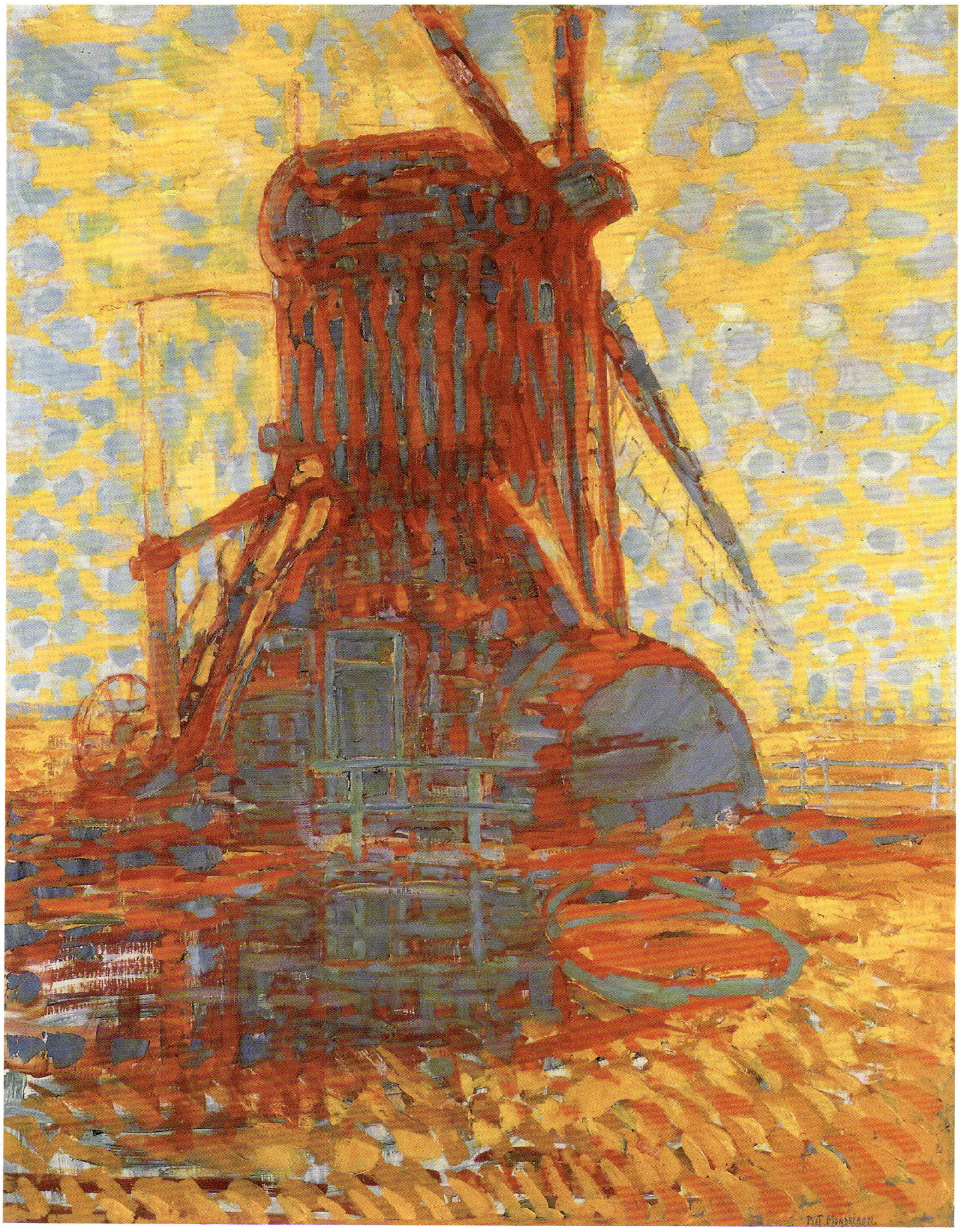

Mill in Sunlight

1908 114 × 87cm [cat.19]

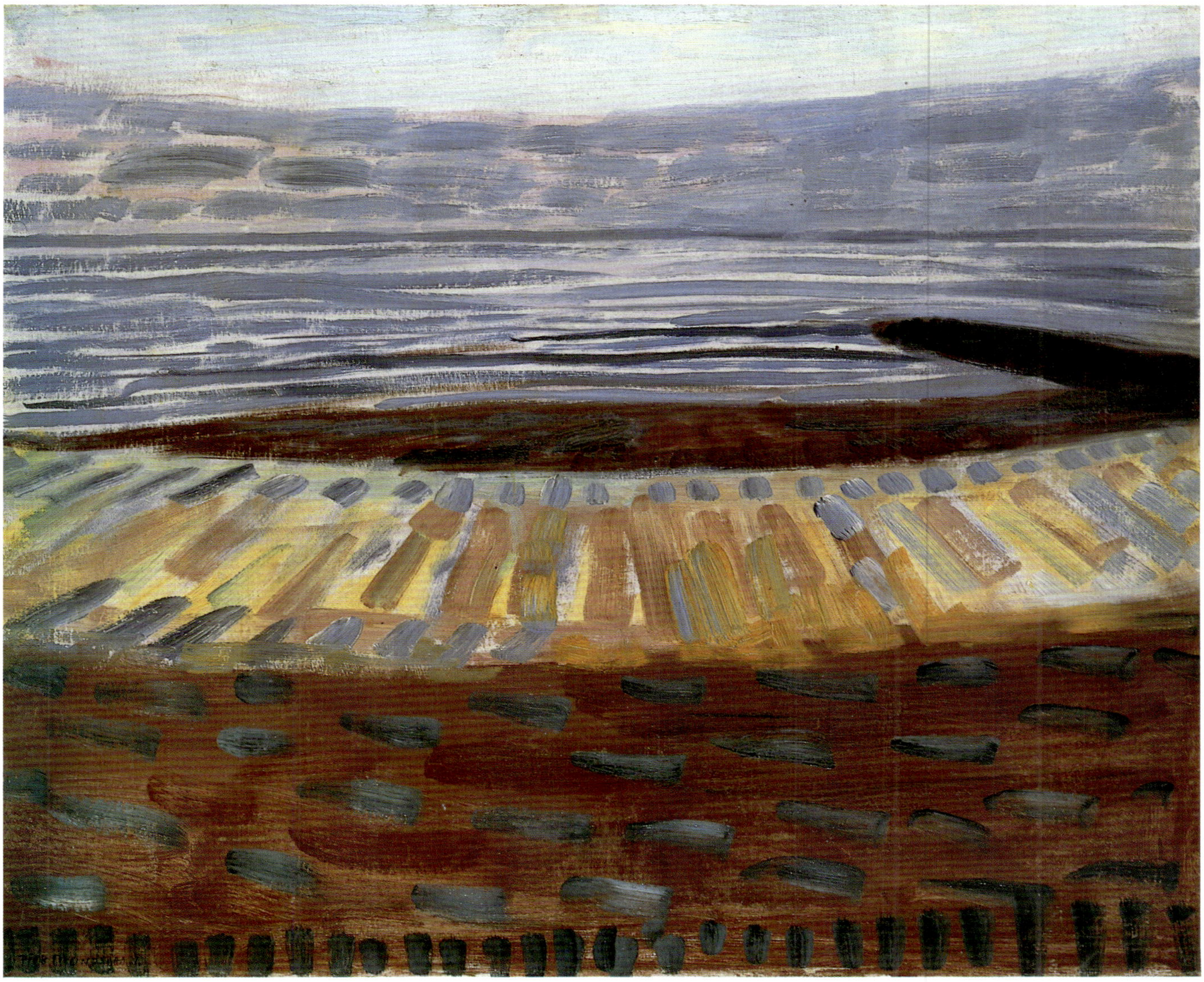

Sea after Sunset

1909 62.5 × 74.5cm [cat.20]

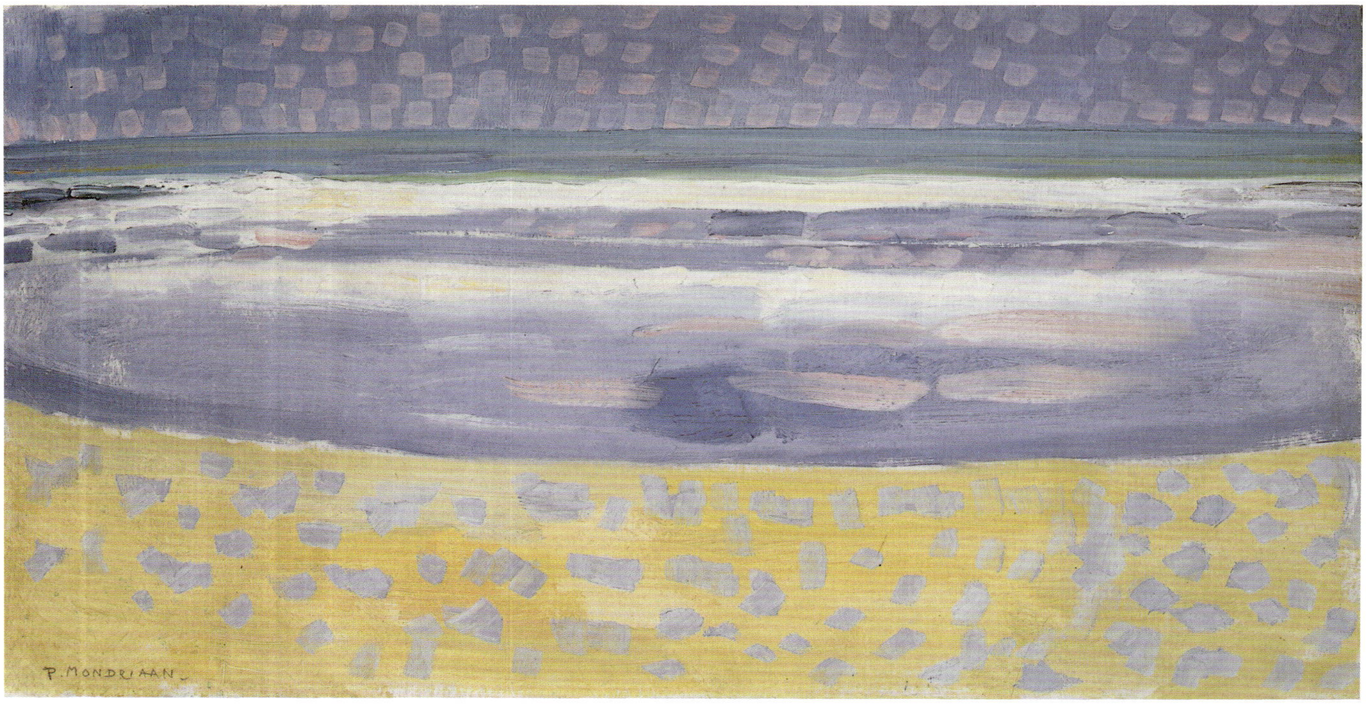

Sea after Sunset

1909 41 × 76cm [cat.21]

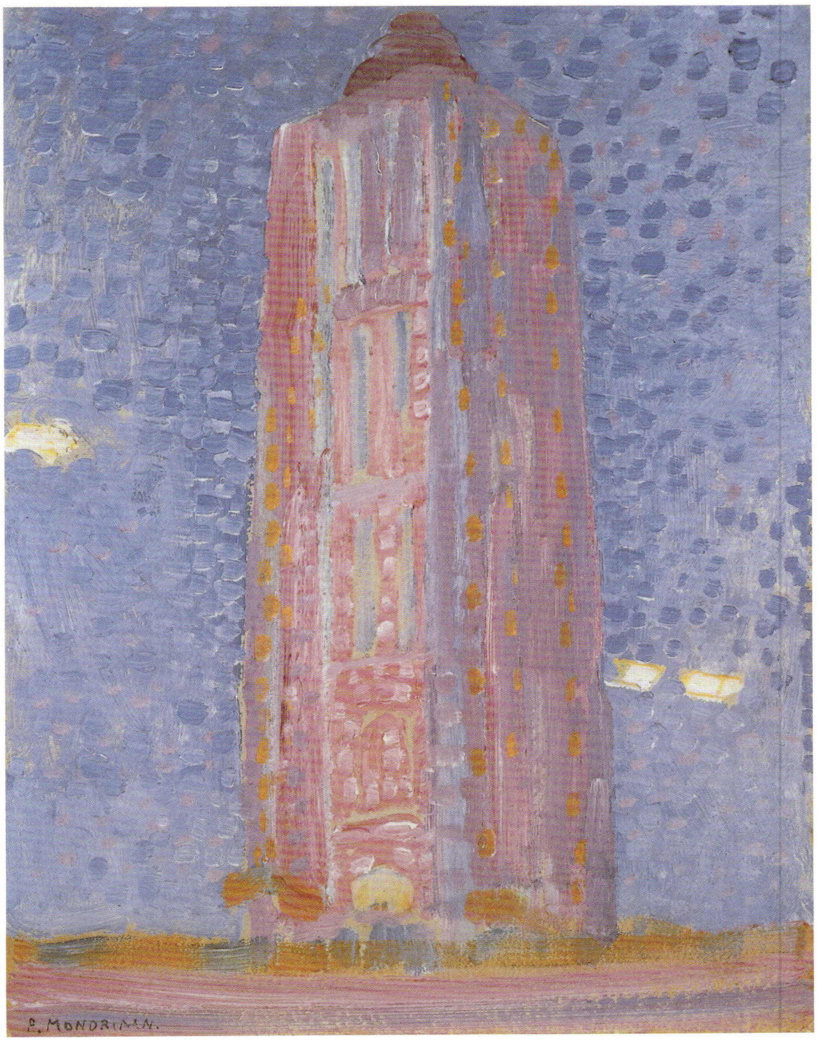

Lighthouse at Westkapelle

1909 39 × 29.5cm [cat.22]

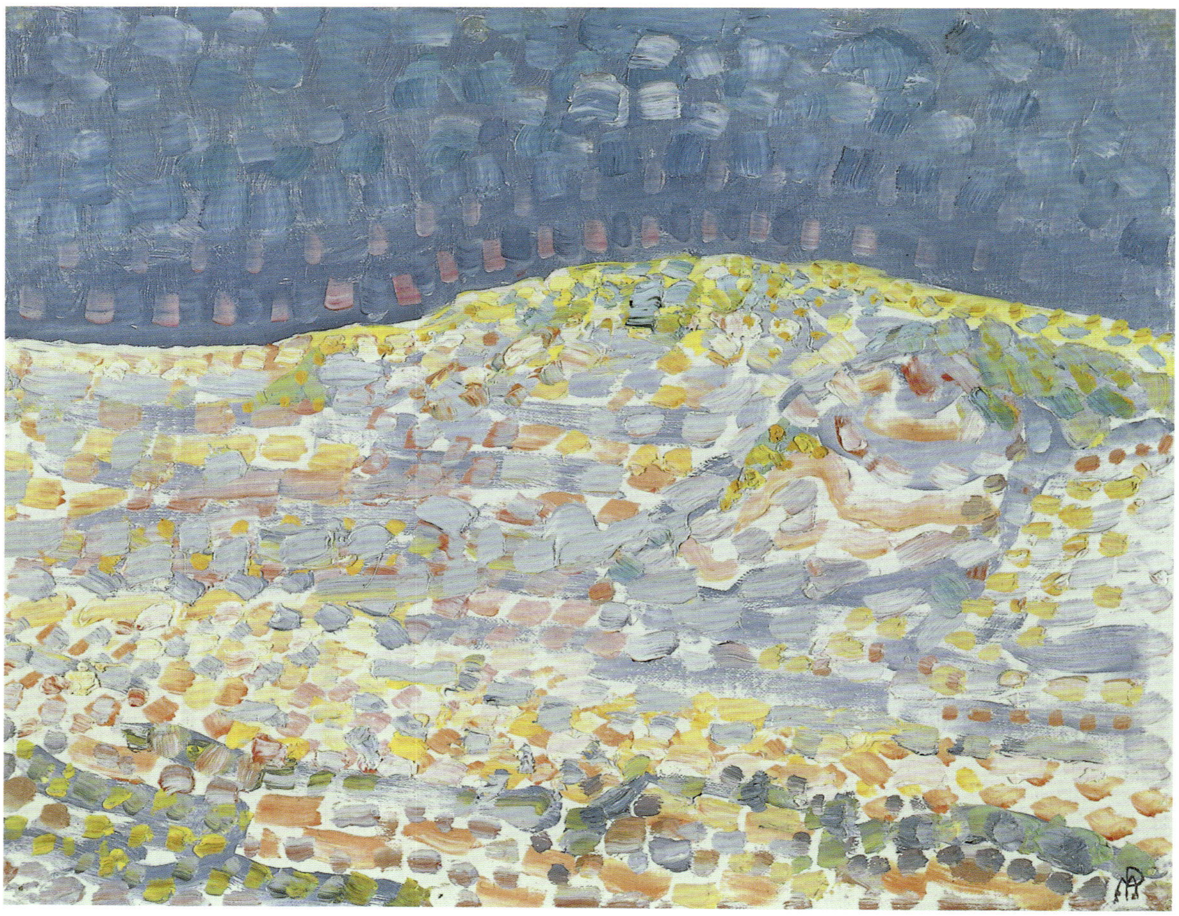

Dune II

1909 37.5 × 46.5cm [cat.23]

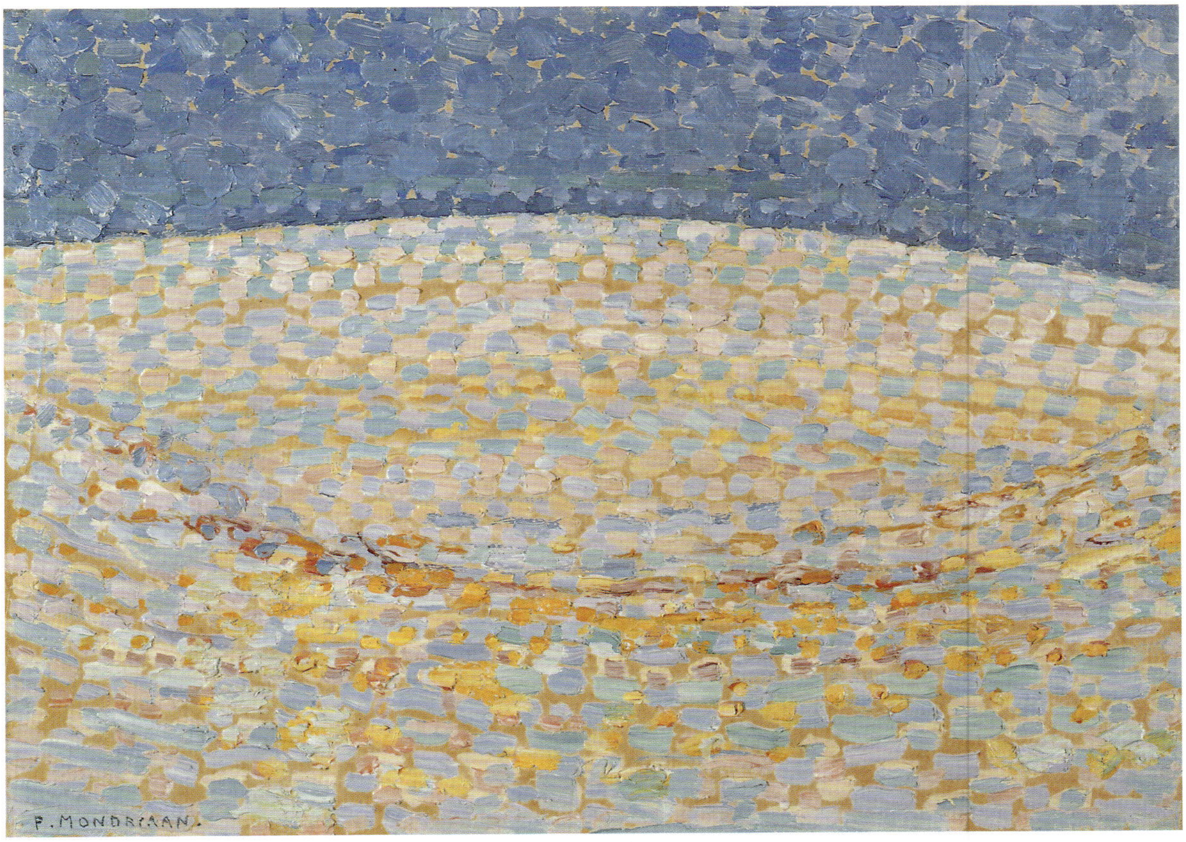

Dune III

1909 29.5 × 39cm [cat.24]

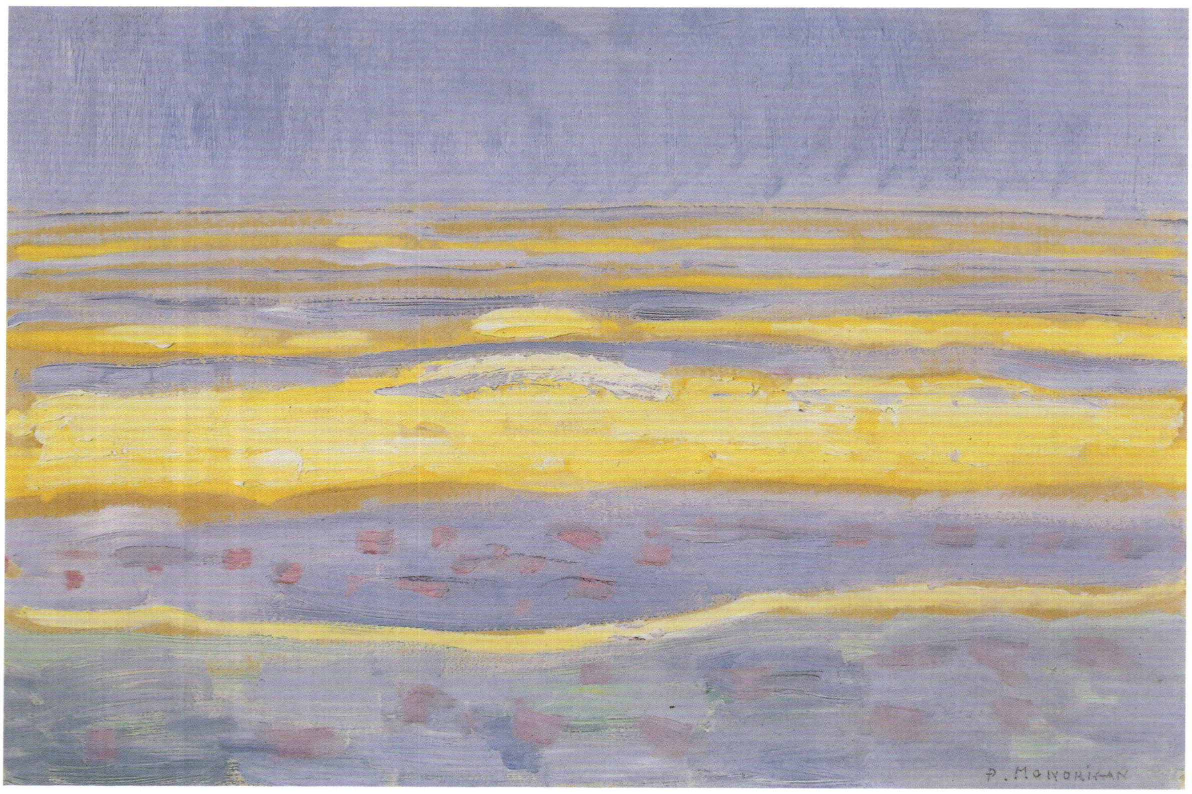

Seascape

1909 34.5 × 50.5cm [cat.25]

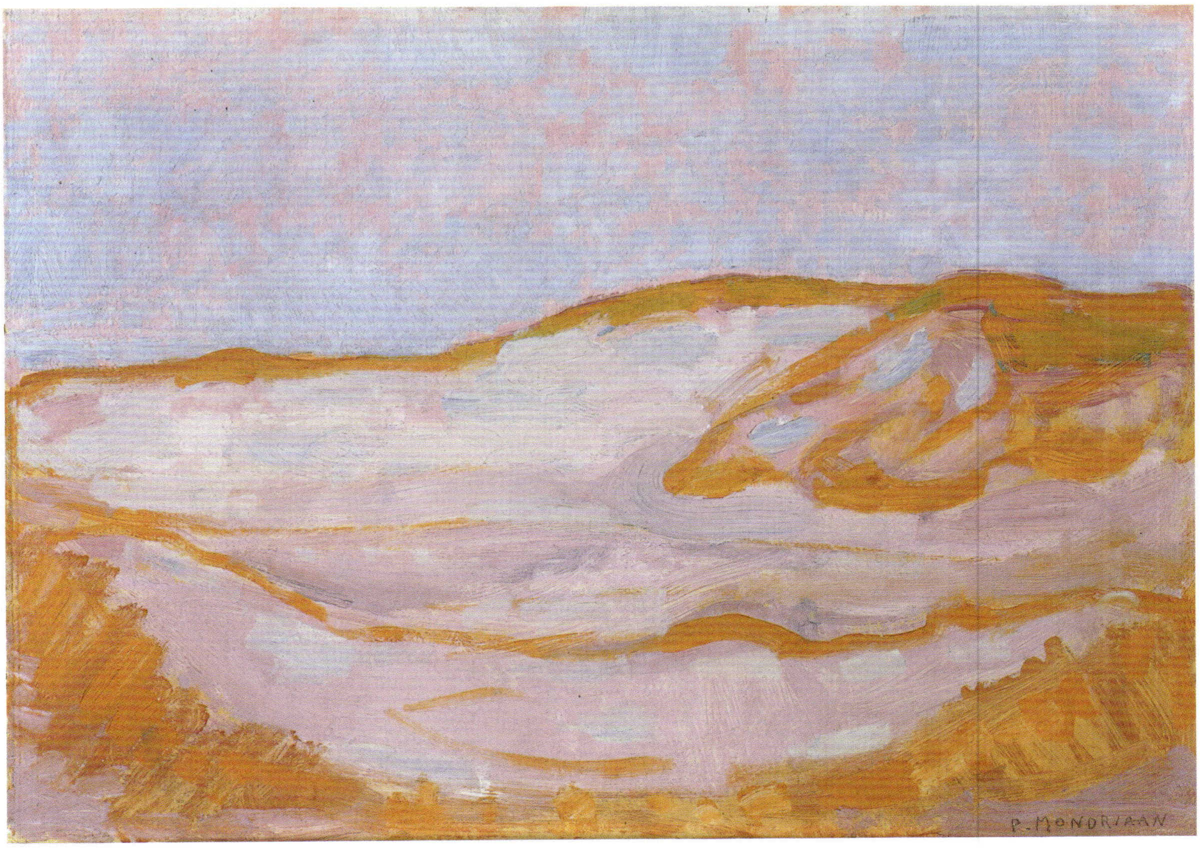

Dune IV

1909–10 33 × 46cm [cat.26]

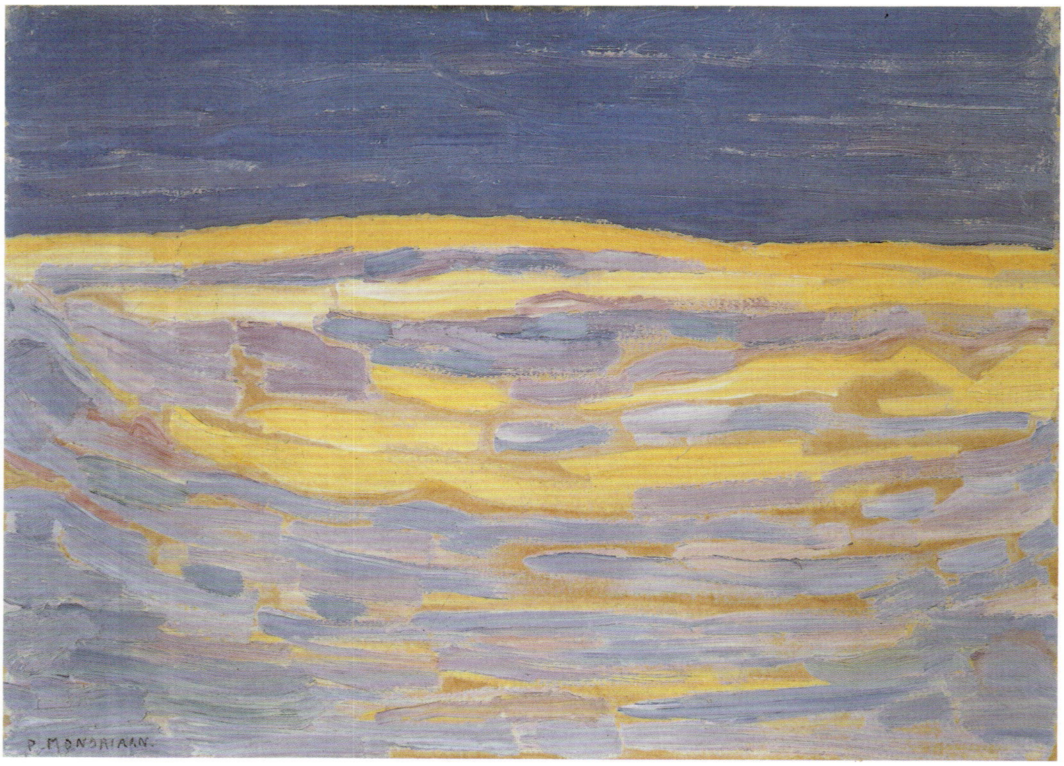

Dune I

1909 30 × 40cm [cat.27]

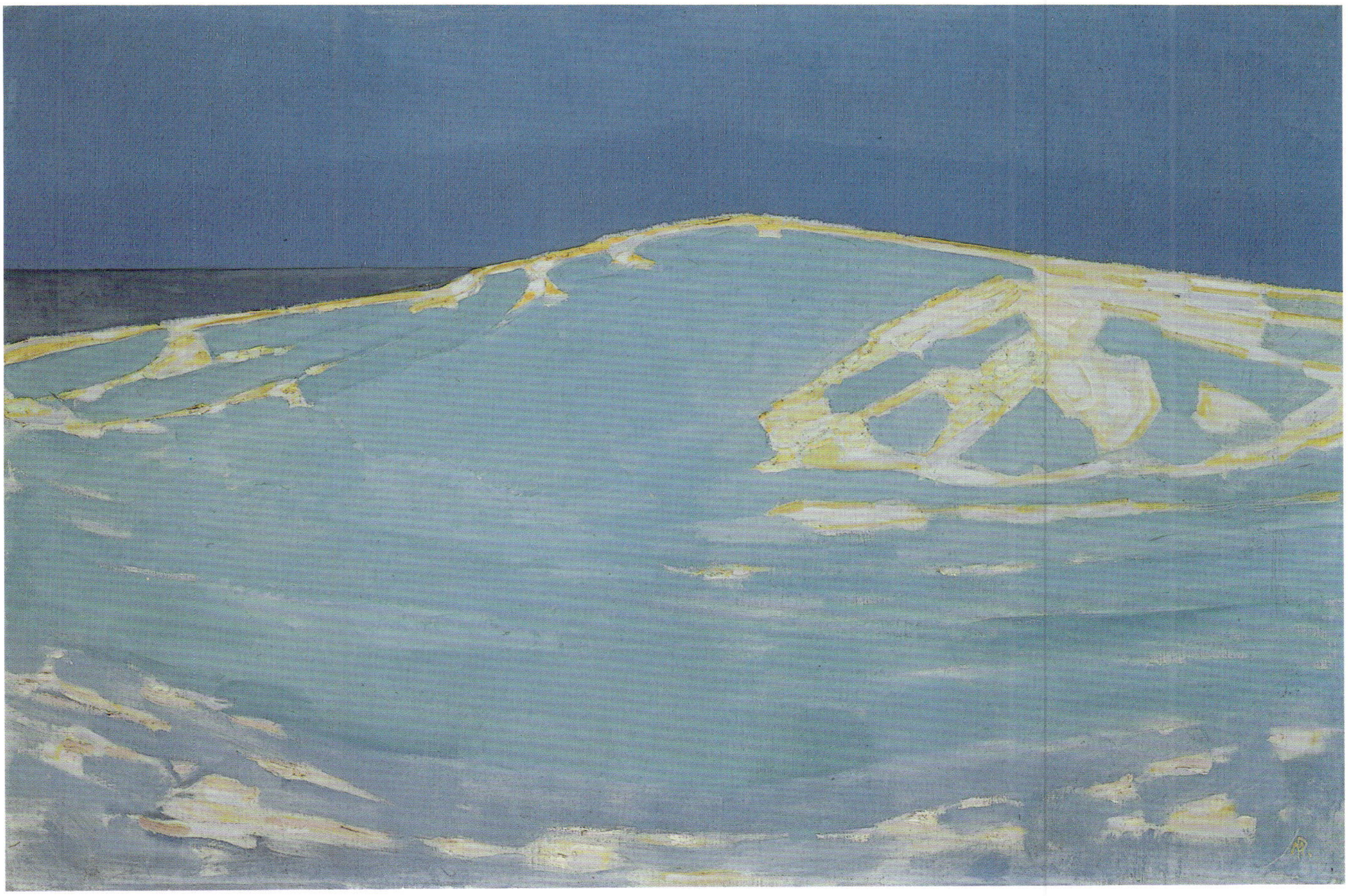

Dune V

1909–10 65.5 × 96cm [cat.28]

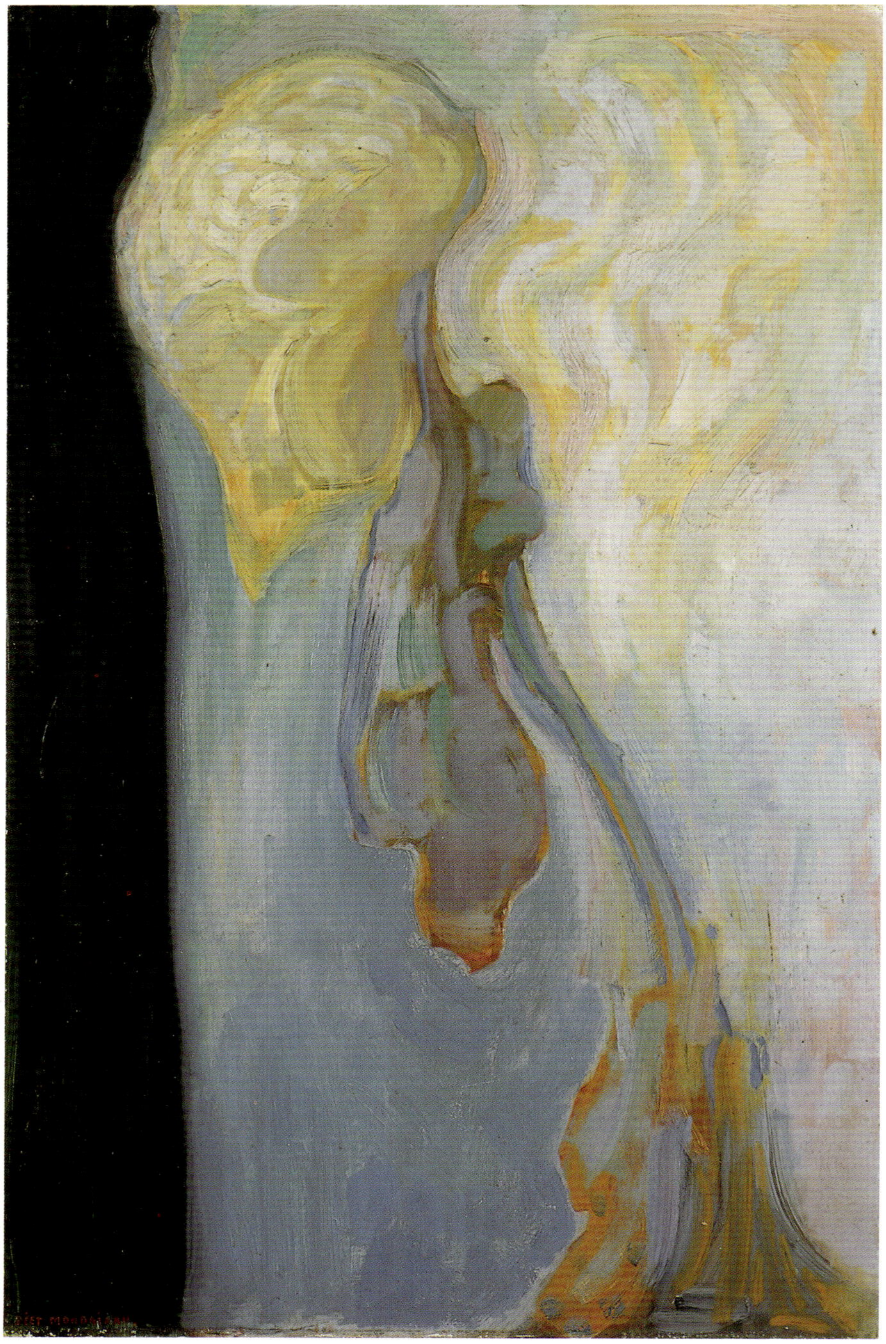

Dying Chrysanthemum

1908 84.5 × 54cm [cat.29]

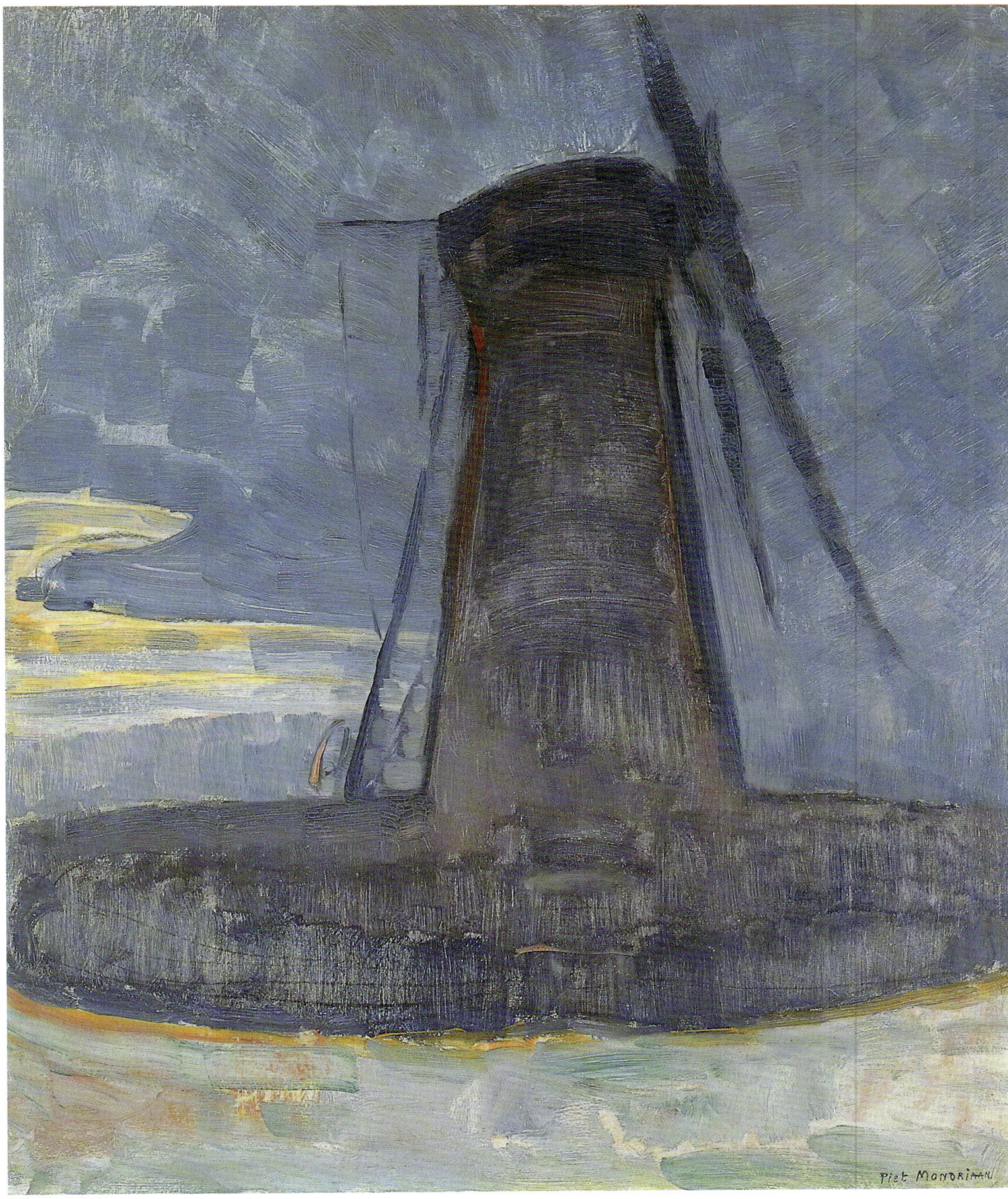

Mill at Domburg

1909 76.5 × 63.5cm [cat.30]

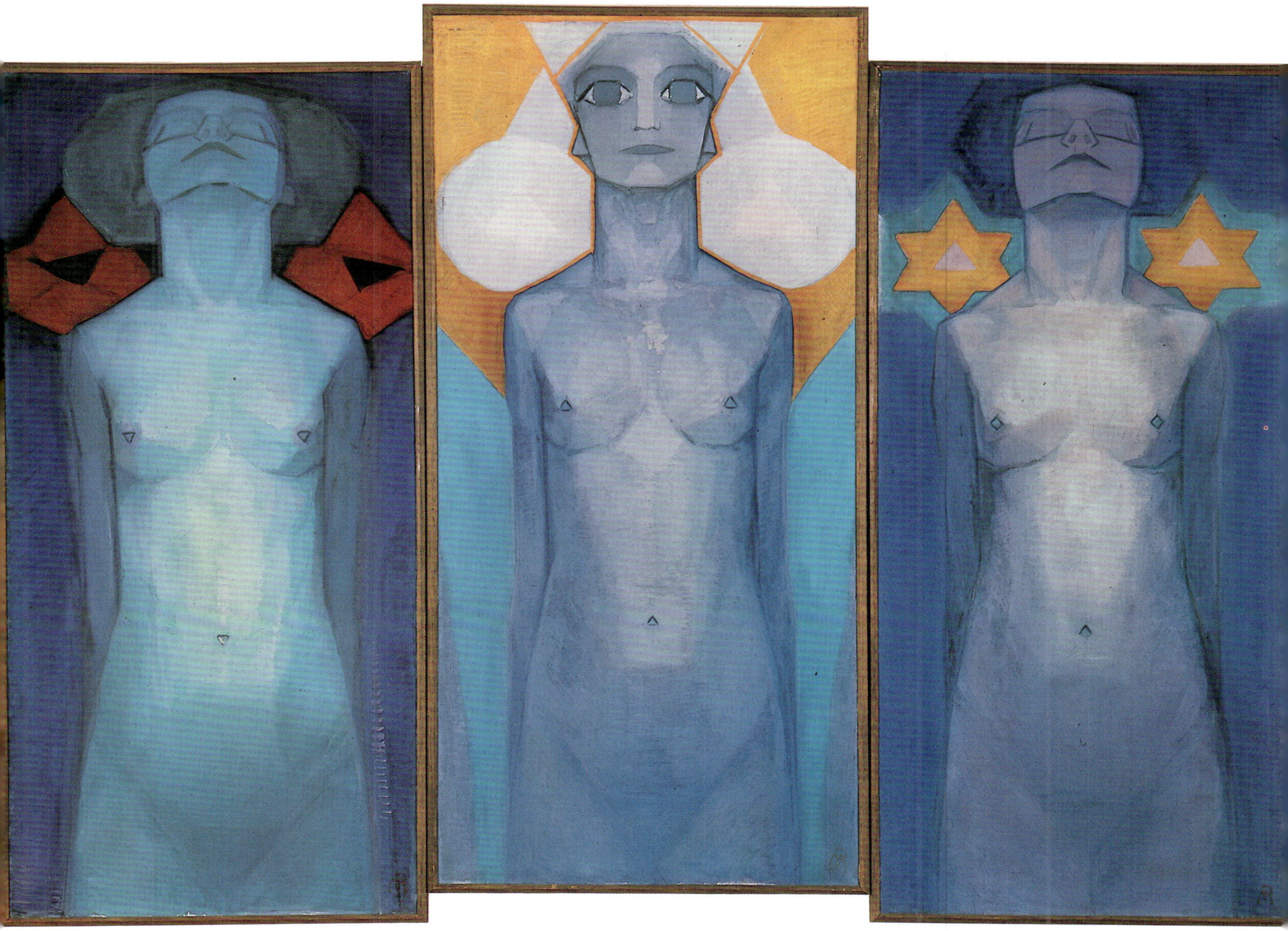

Evolution

1910–11 3 sections 181.8 × 87.8cm, 187.1 × 90.6cm, 181.8 × 87.8cm [cat.31]

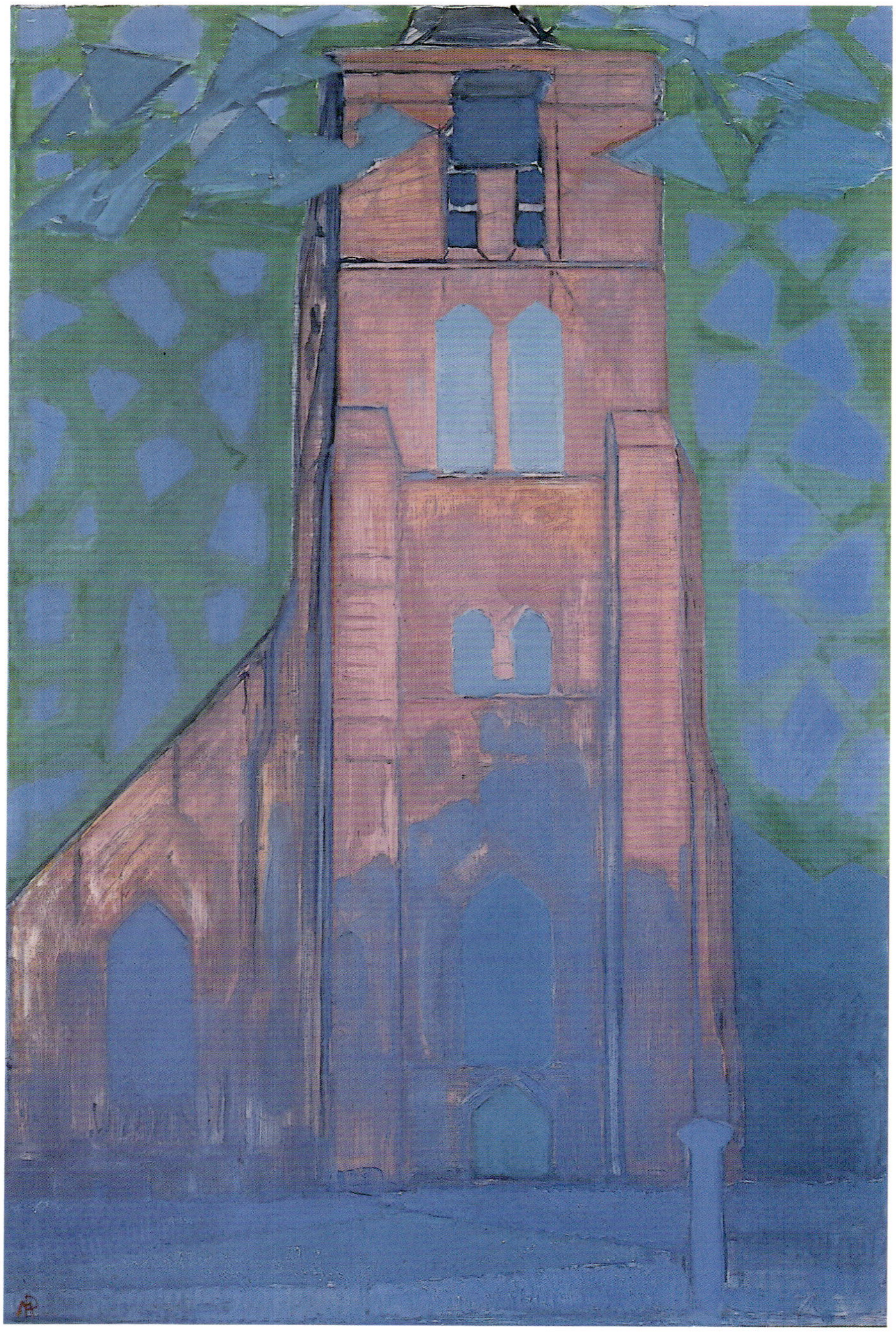

Church at Domburg

1910–11 114 × 75cm [cat.32]

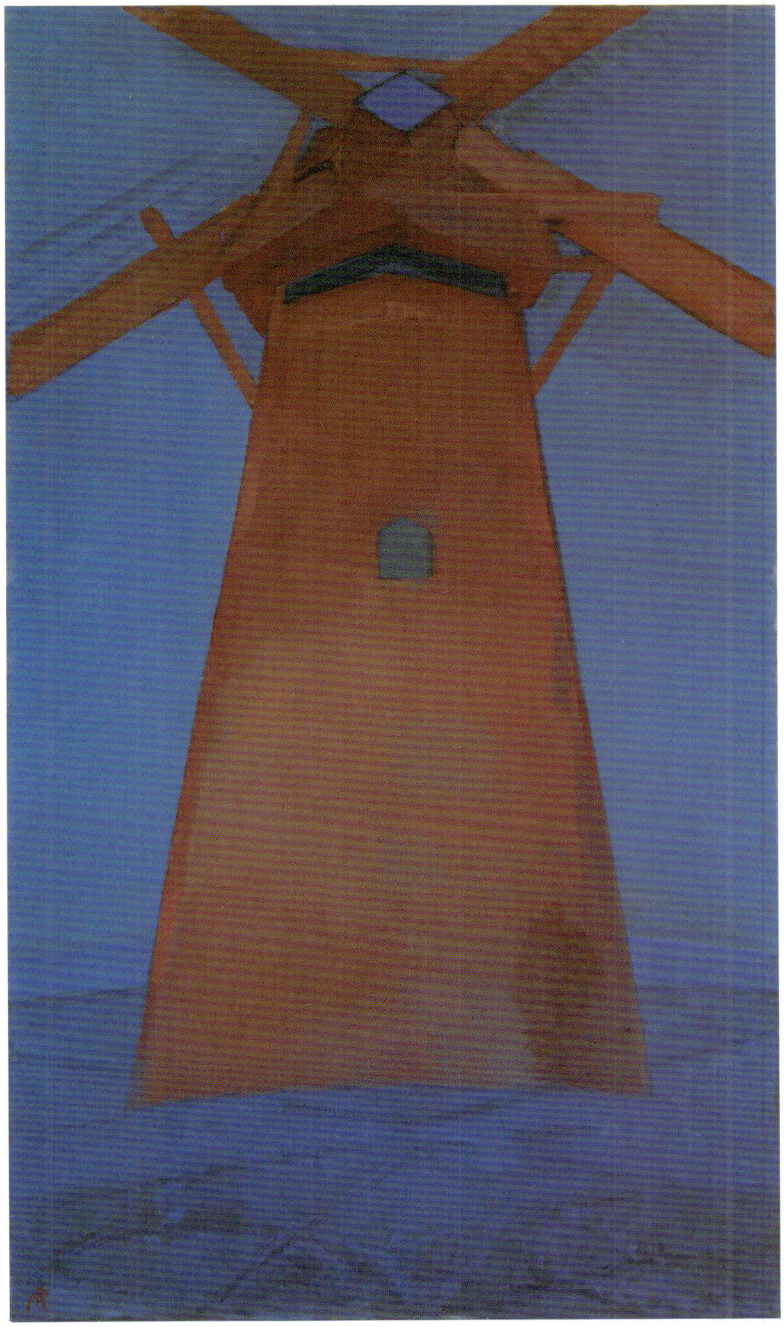

Red Mill

1910–11 150 × 86cm [cat.33]

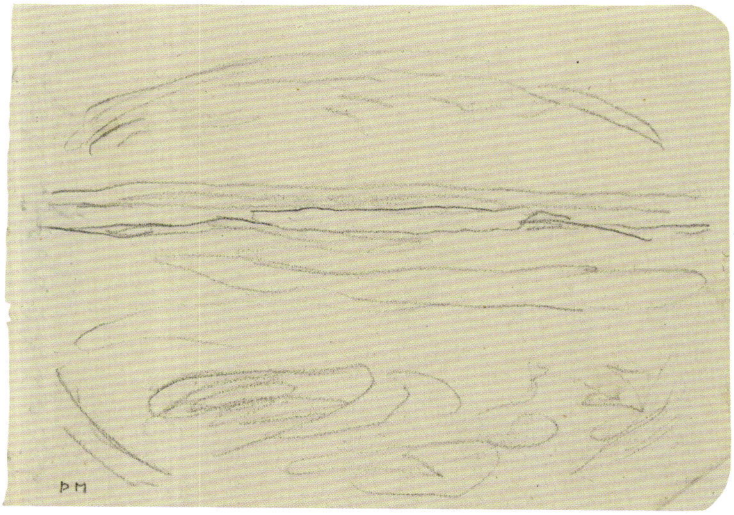

Sea

1913–14 11.4 × 15.8cm [cat.34]

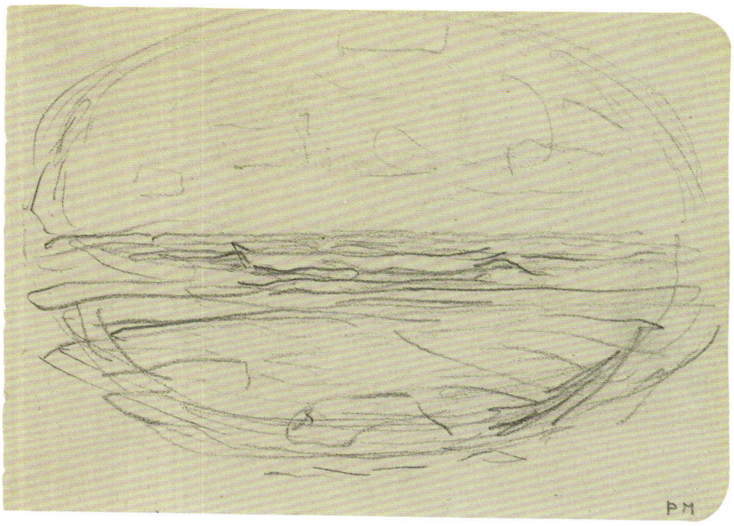

Sea

1914 11.4 × 15.8cm [cat.35]

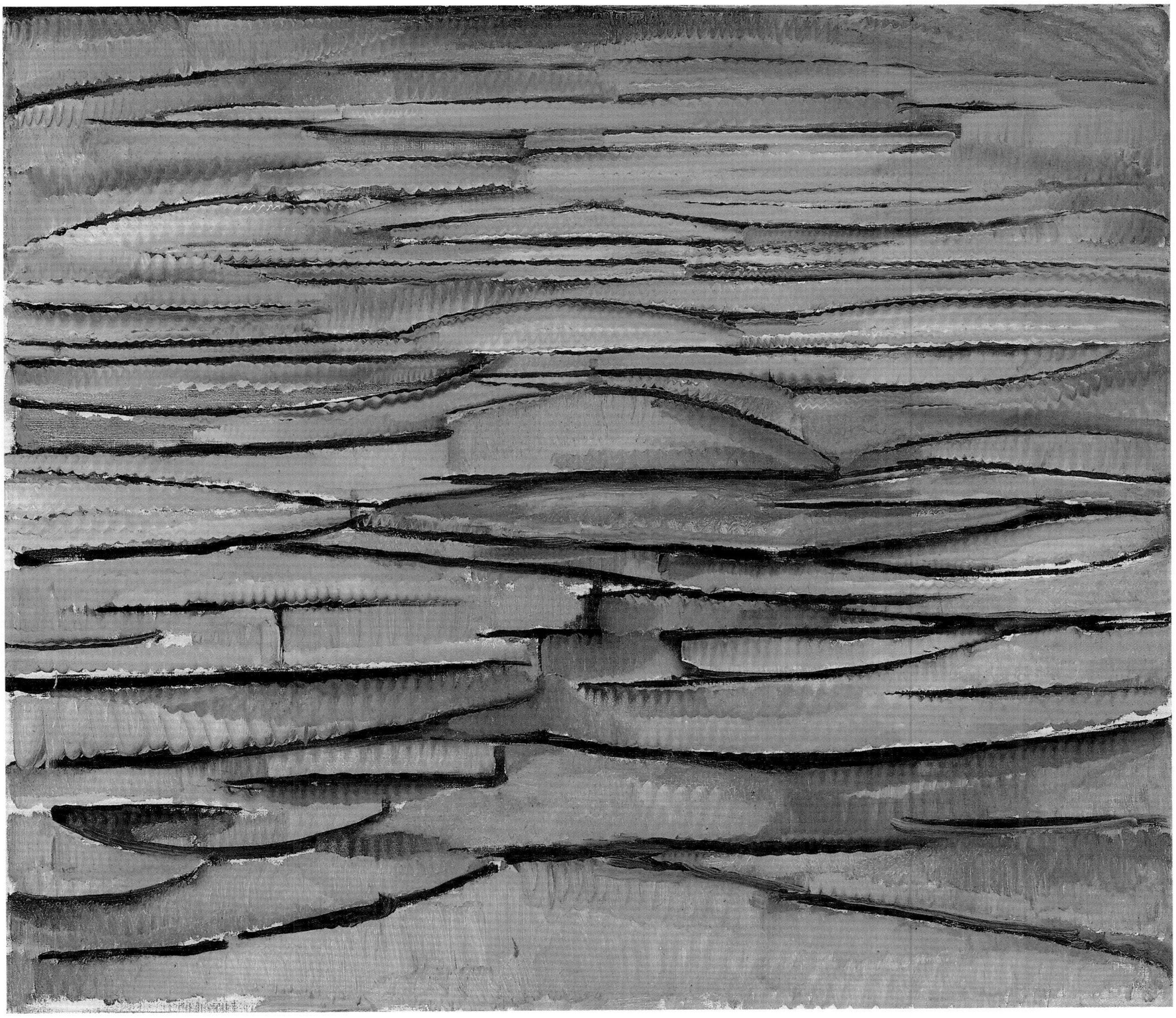

The Sea

1912 82.5 × 92cm [cat.36]

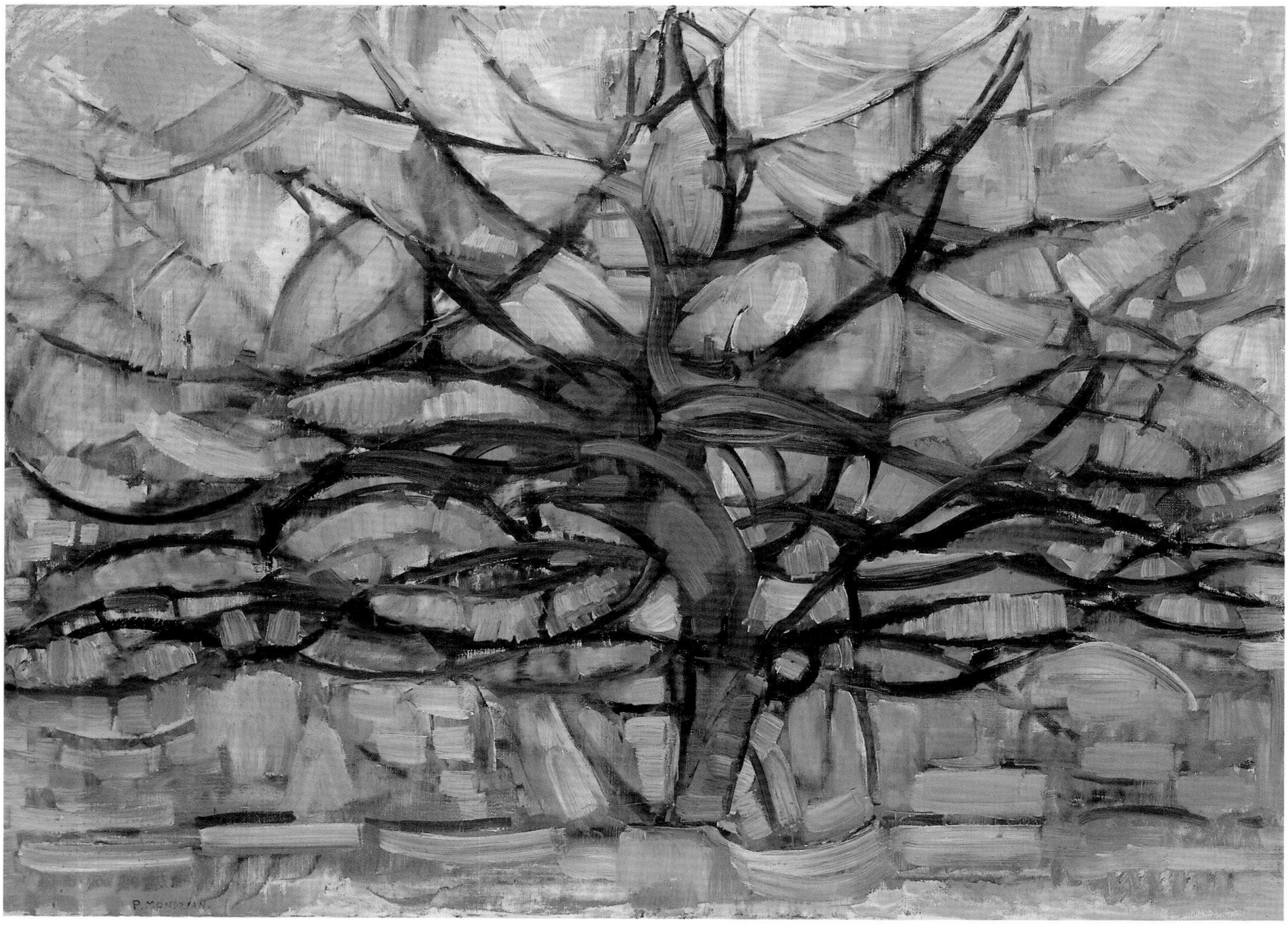

Grey Tree

1912 78.5 × 107.5cm [cat.37]

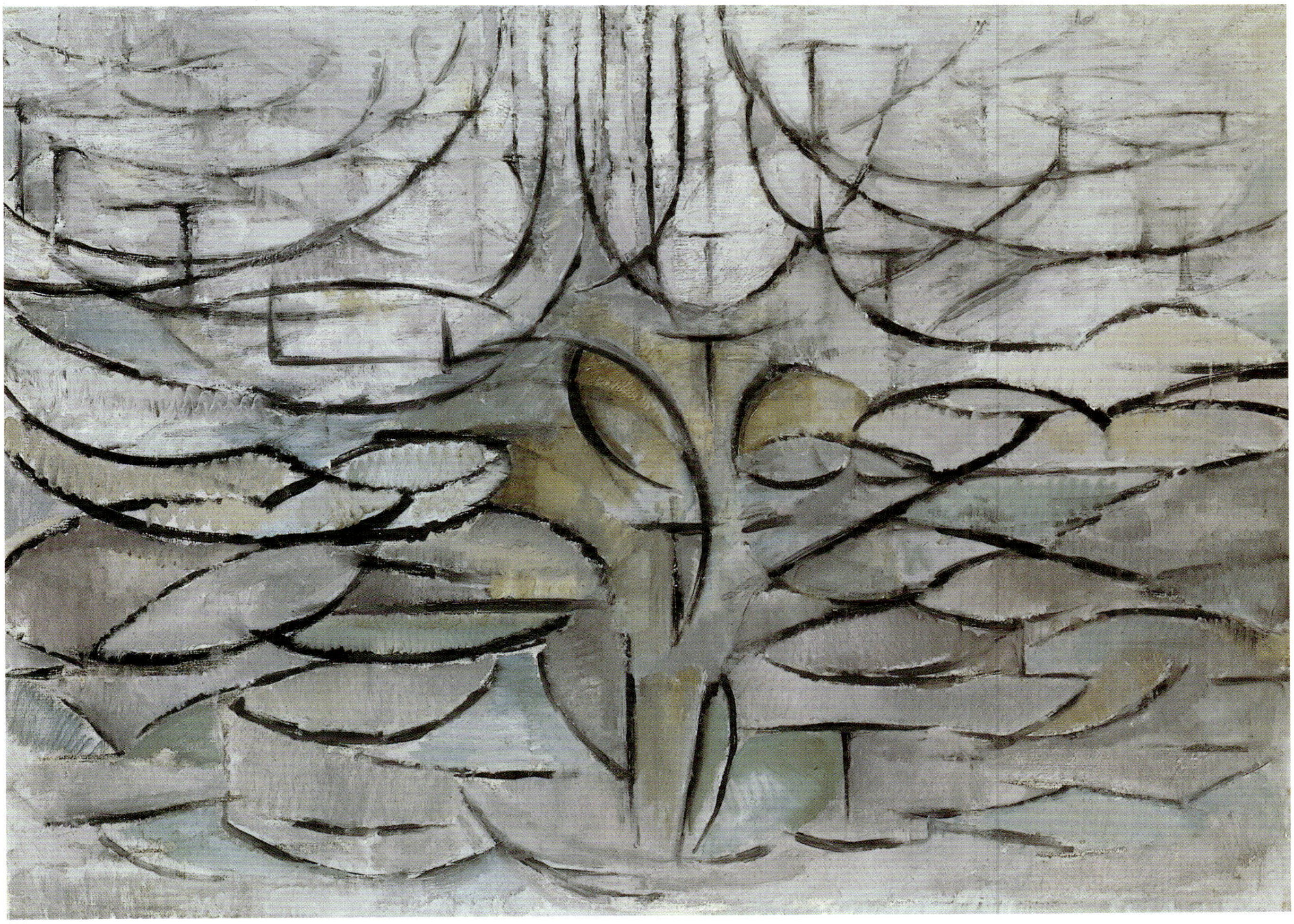

Flowering Appletree

1912 78 × 106cm [cat.38]

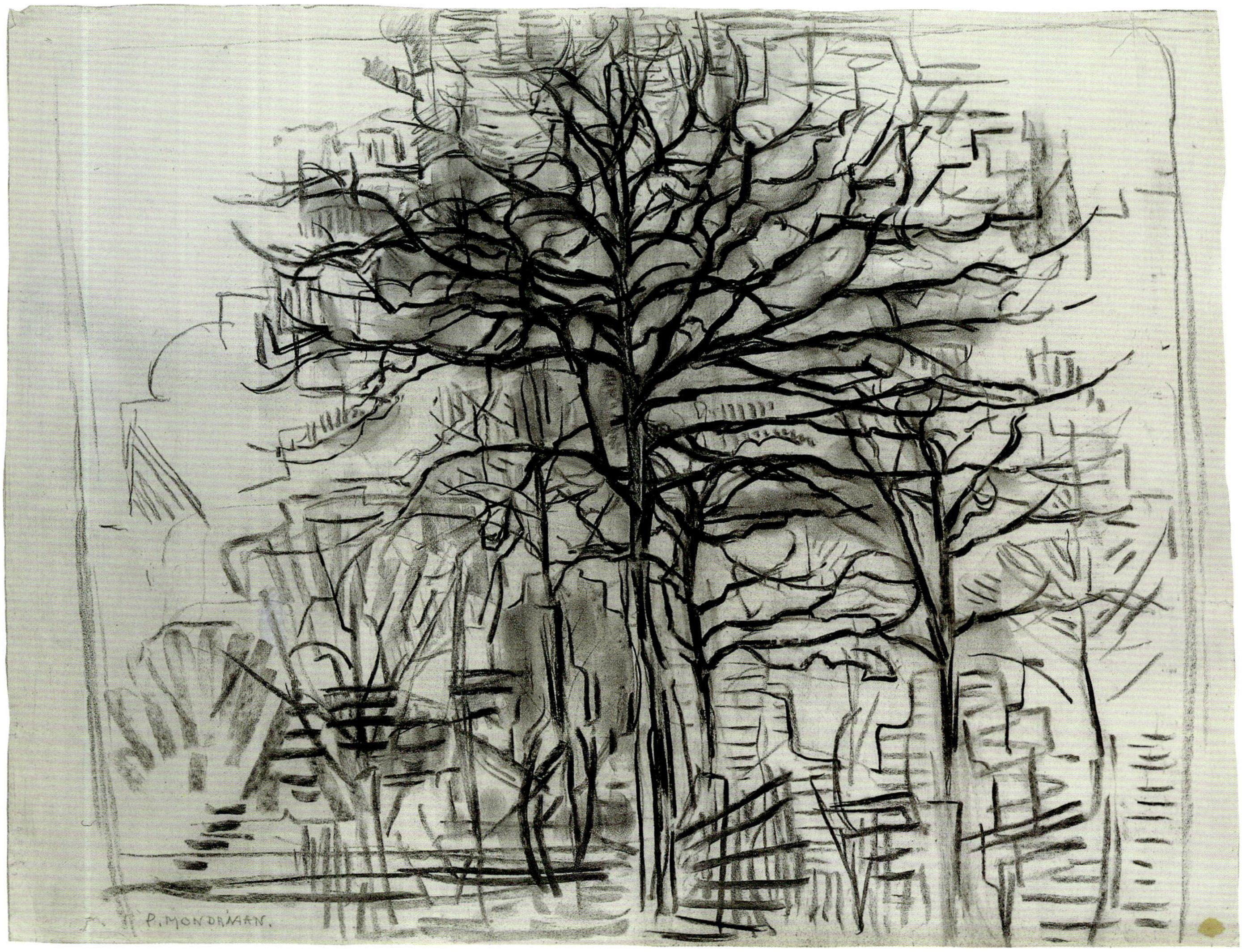

Studies of Trees II

1913 65.5 × 87.5cm [cat.39]

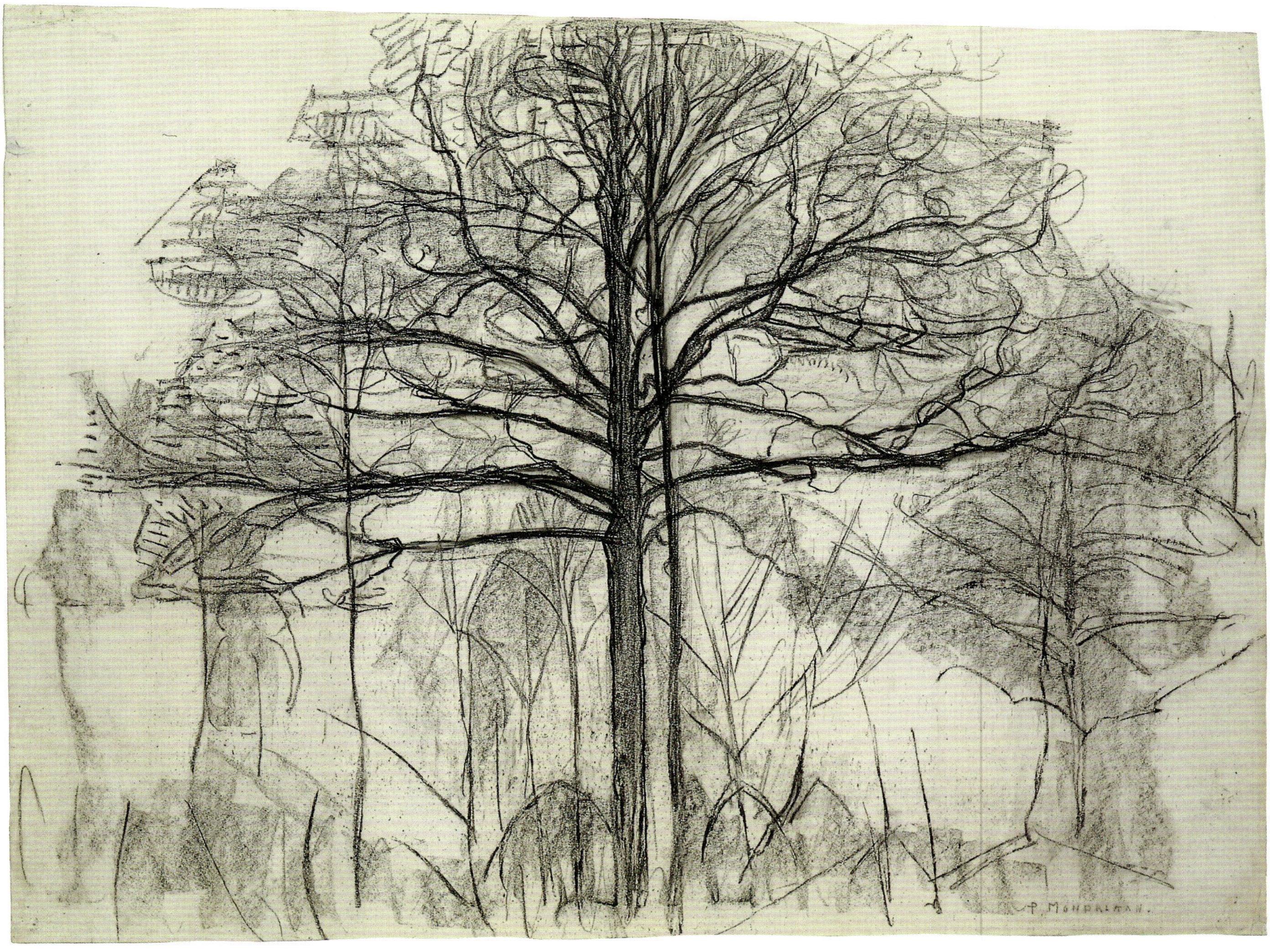

Study of Trees I

1912 65 × 89cm [cat.40]

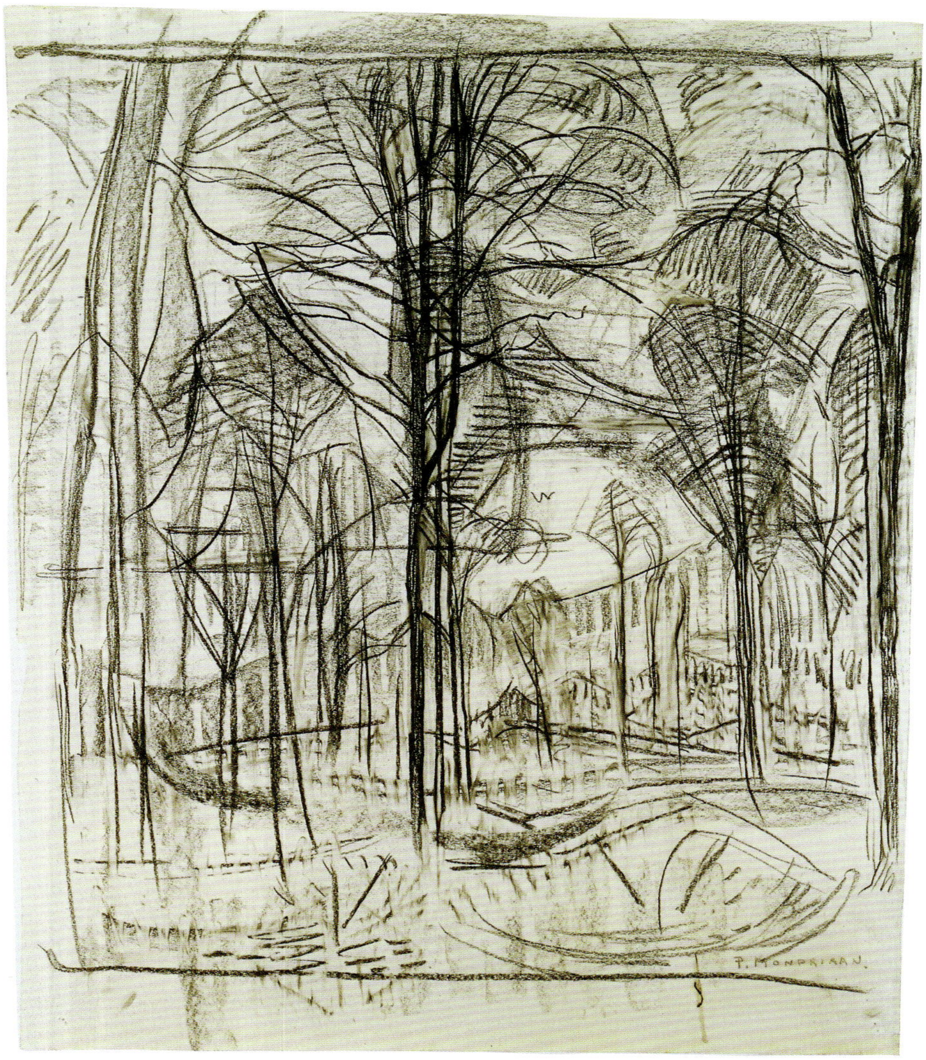

Forest

1912 73 × 63cm [cat.41]

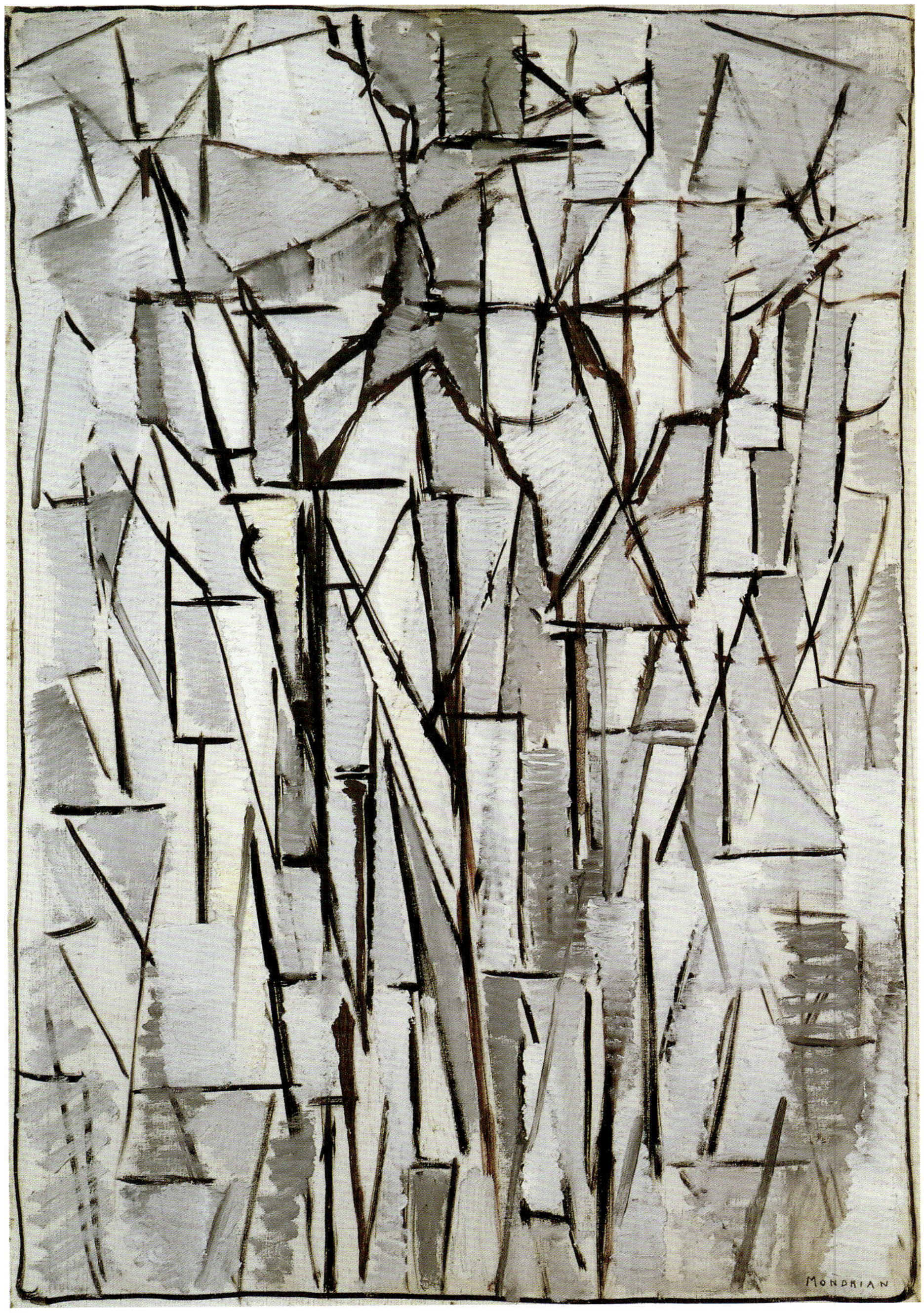

Composition Trees II

1912 98 × 65cm [cat.42]

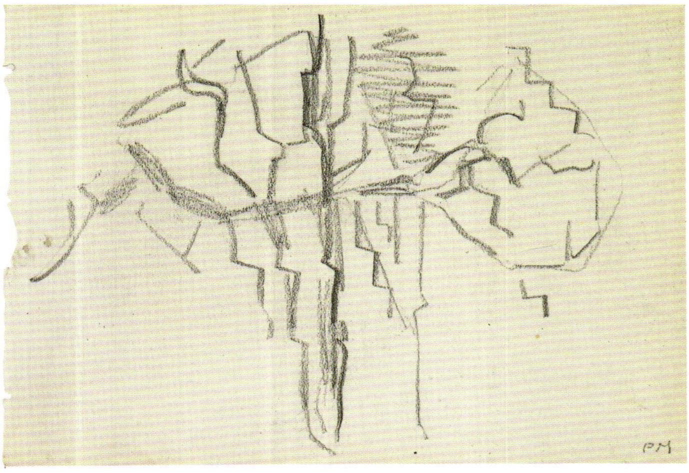

Tree (study)

1913 13.4 × 17.8cm [cat.43]

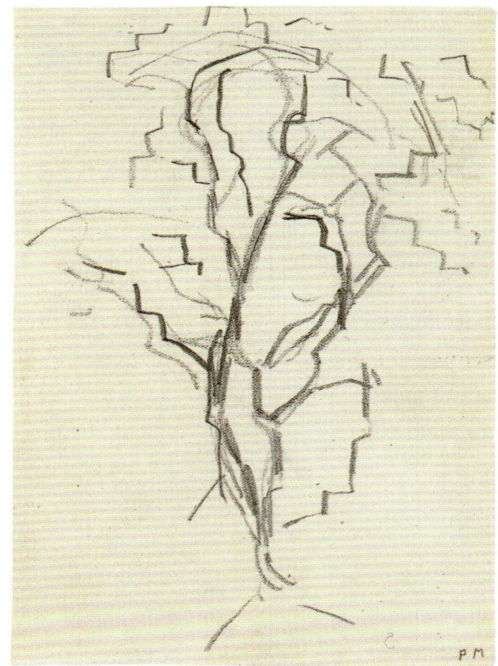

Tree (study)

1913 17 × 12.3cm [cat.44]

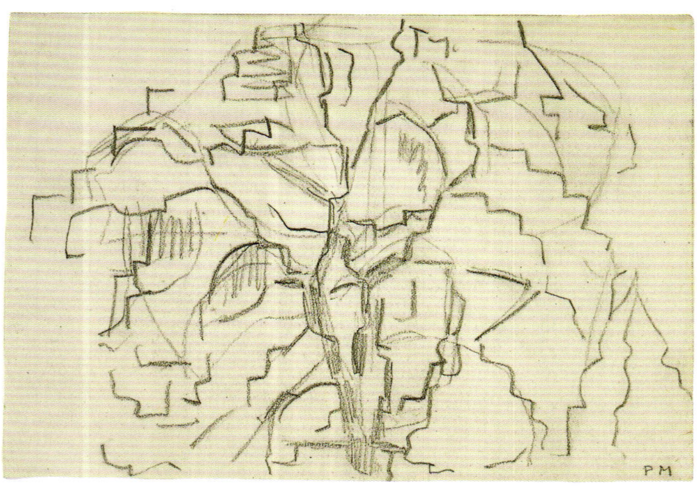

Study of a Tree

1913 12.4 × 17.8cm [cat.45]

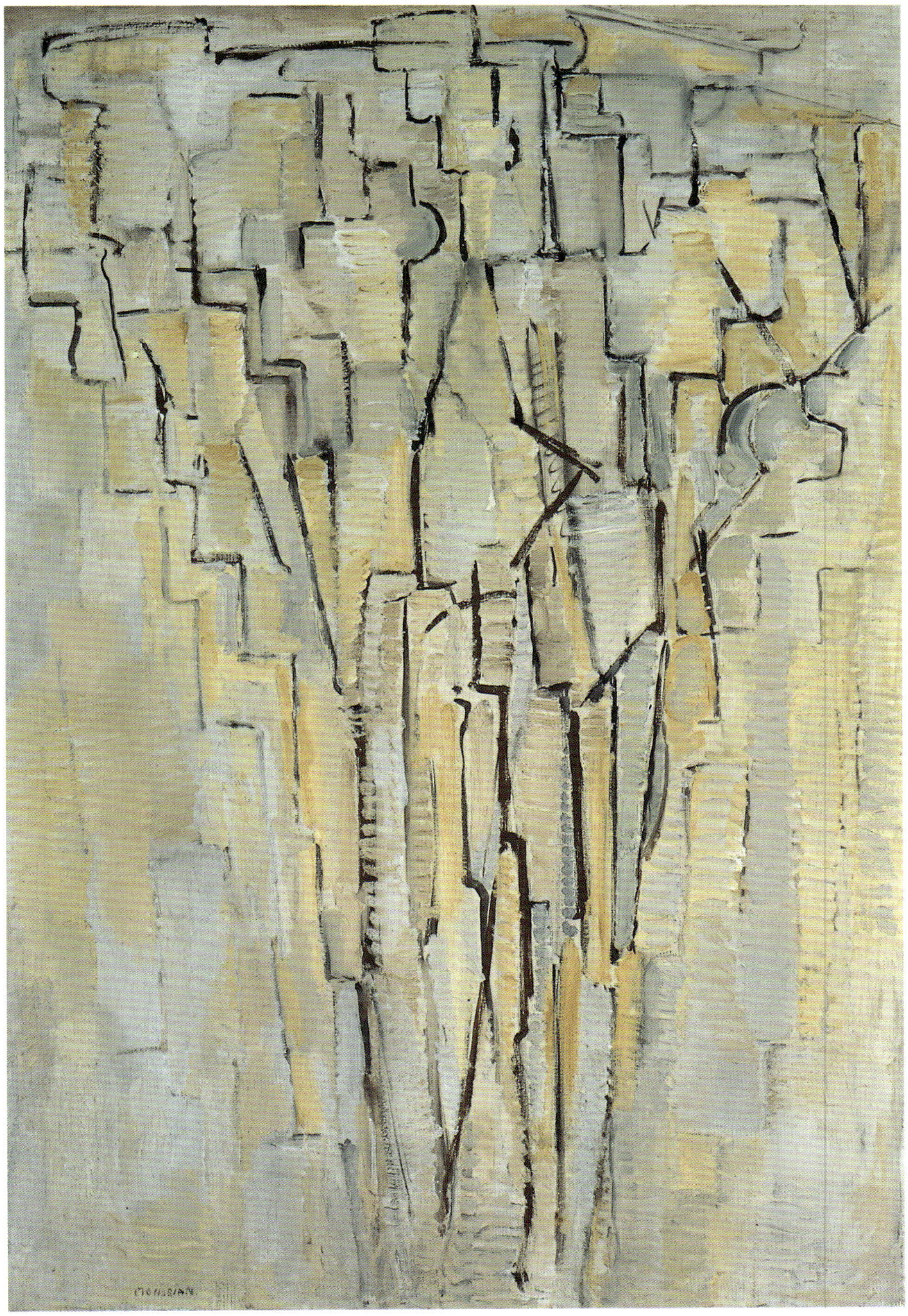

Tree

c.1913 100.3 × 67.3cm [cat.46]

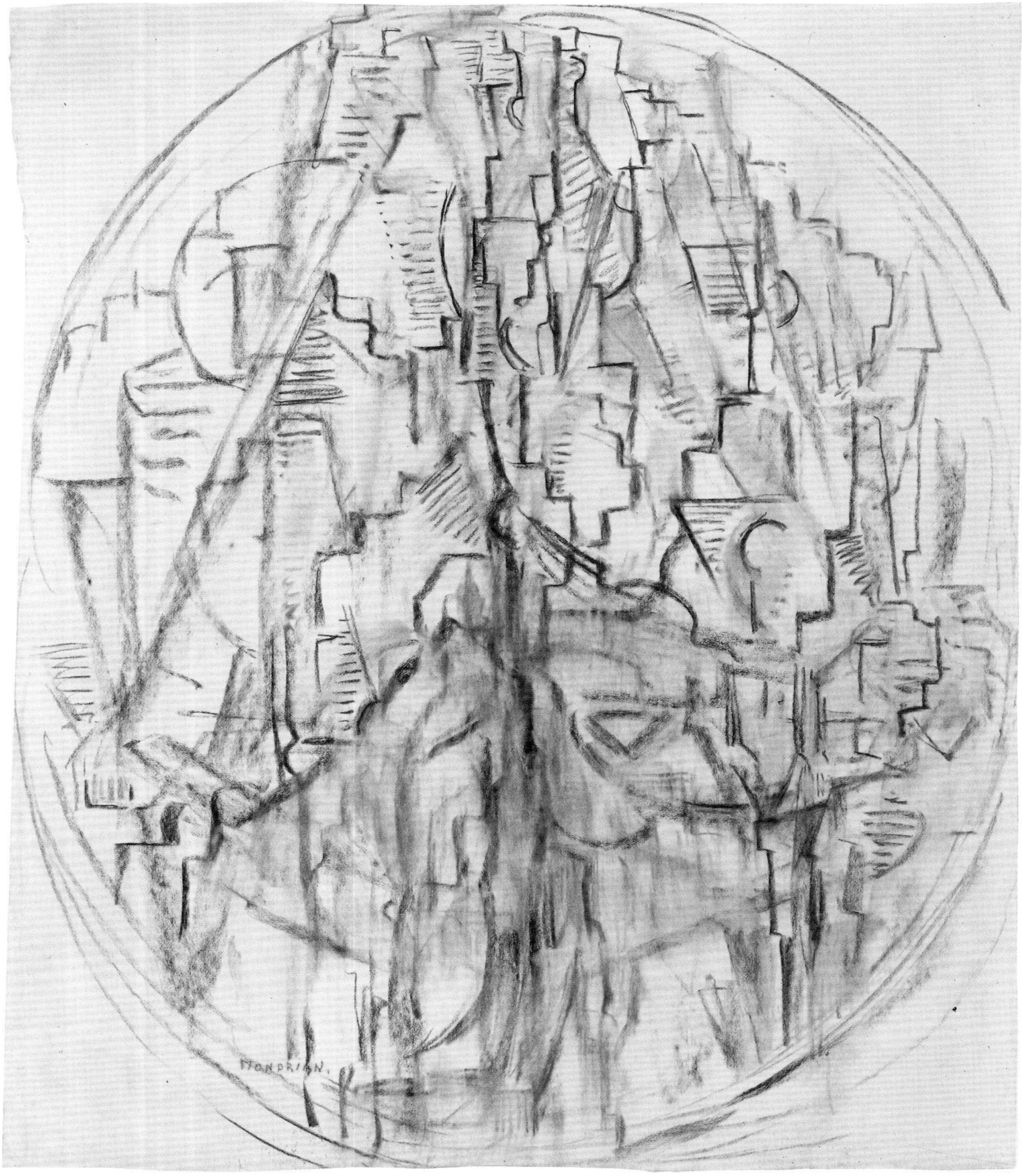

Composition in Oval

1913 85 × 70cm [cat.47]

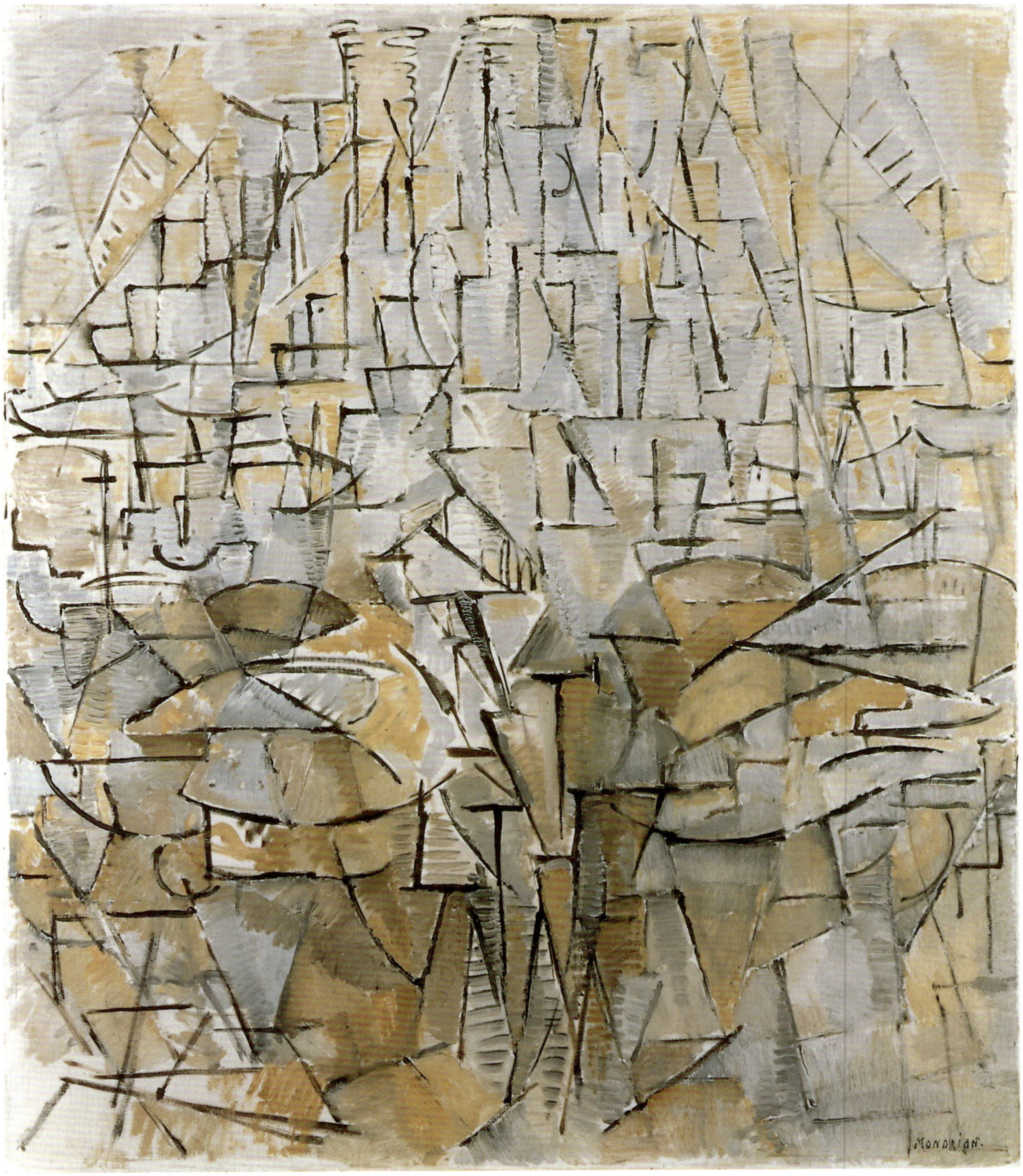

Composition III in Colour

1913 95 × 80cm [cat.48]

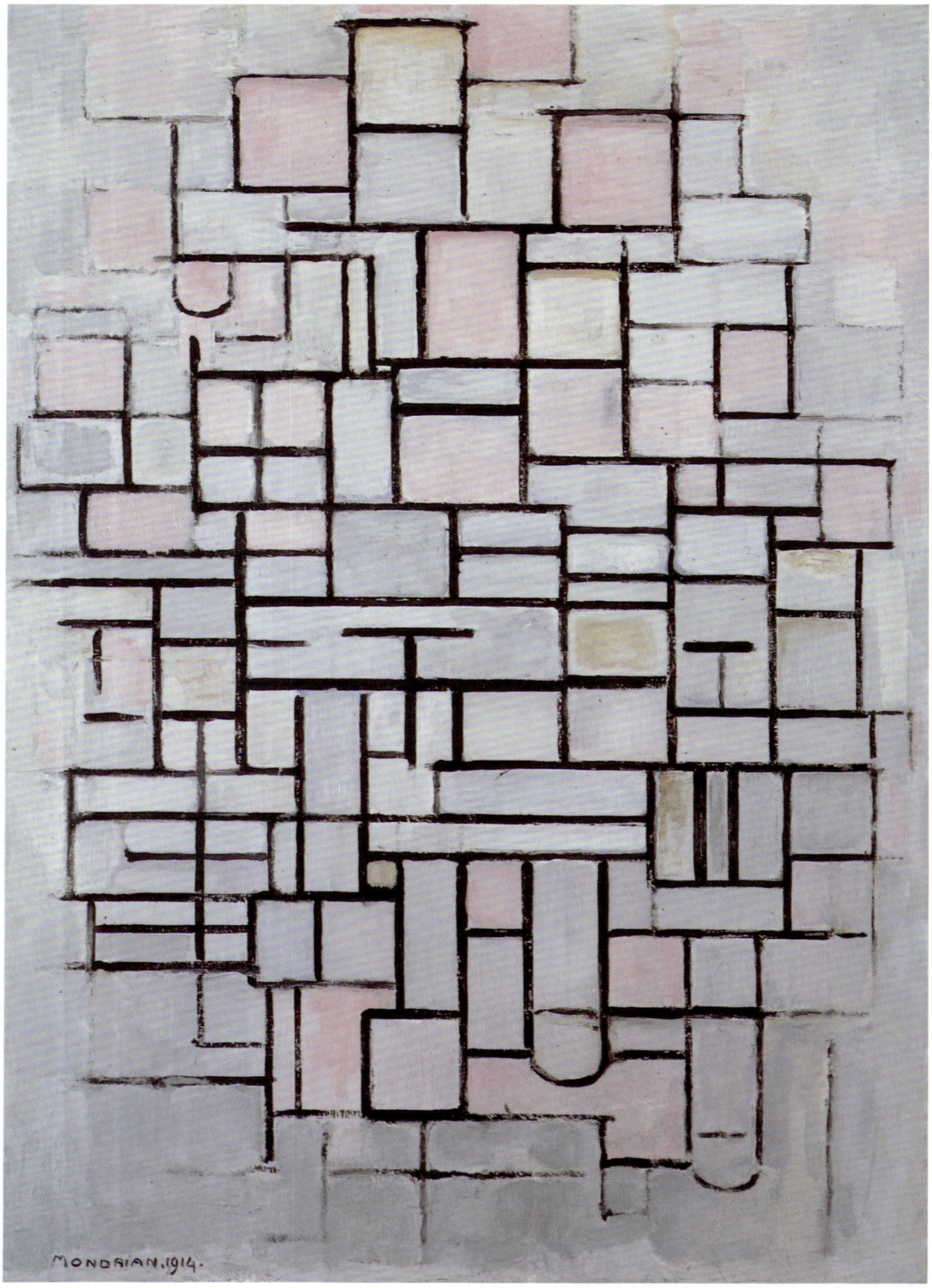

Composition 6

1914 88 × 61cm [cat.49]

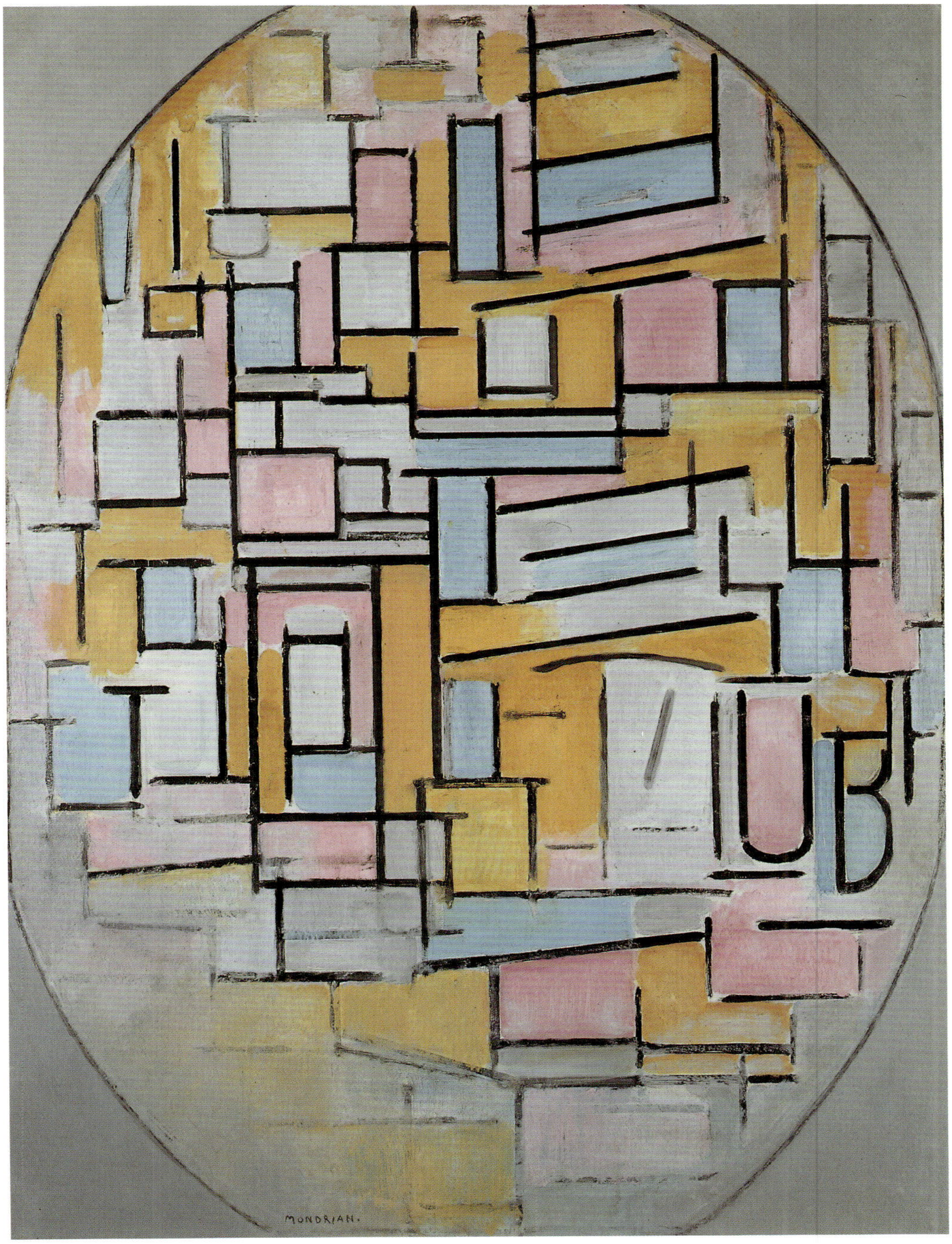

Composition in Oval with Colour Planes

1914 113 × 84.5cm [cat.50]

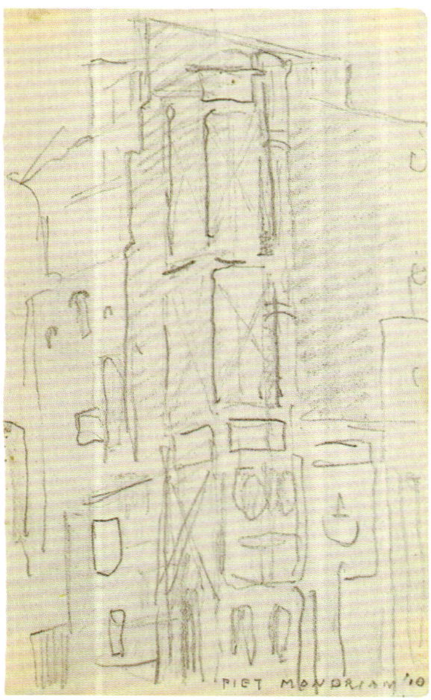

Façade

1912–14 15.8 × 11.4cm [cat.51]

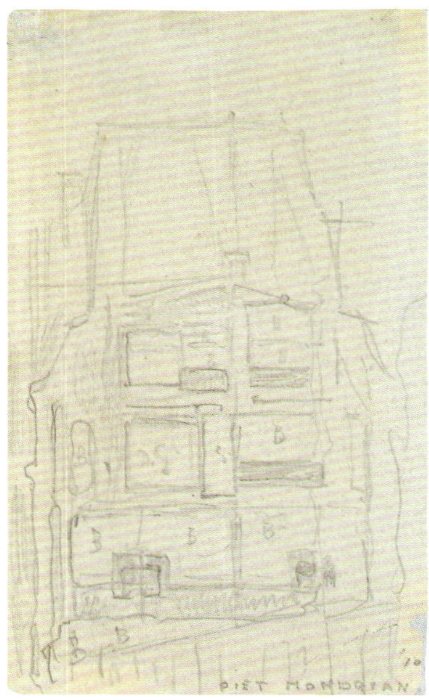

Sketch for 'Blue Façade'

1914 17.2 × 10.5cm [cat.52]

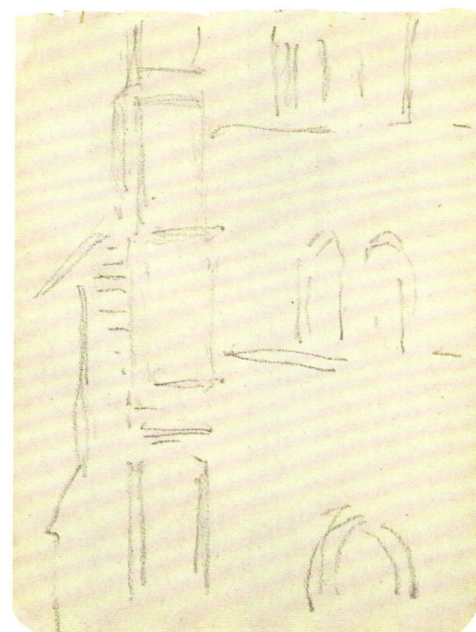

Church at Domburg

1913–14 17.2 × 10.5cm [cat.53]

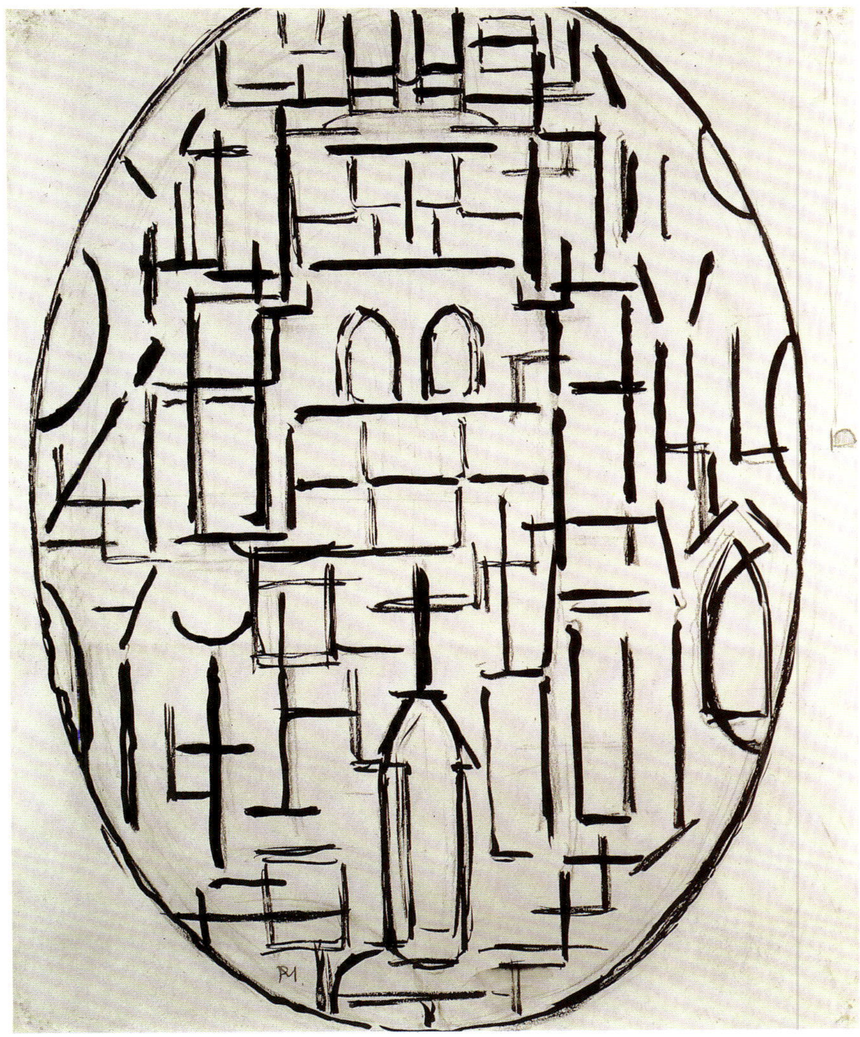

Church at Domburg

1914 63 × 50cm [cat.54]

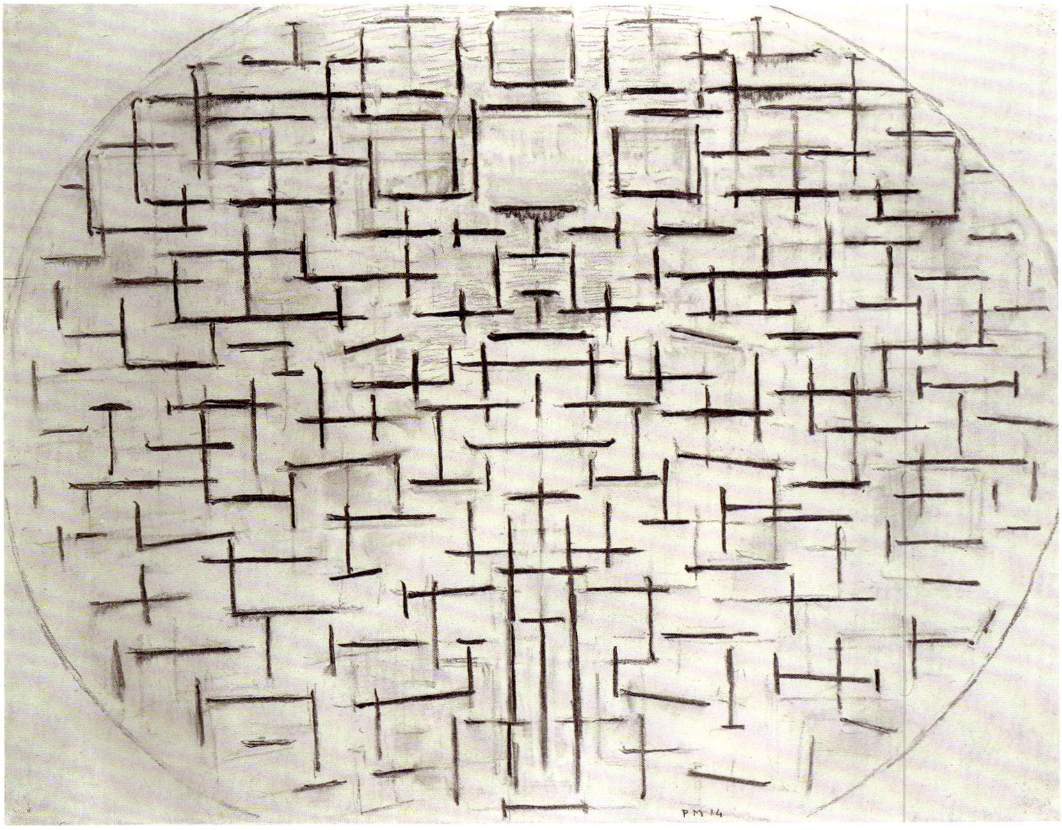

Sea, Pier and Ocean

1914 51 × 63cm [cat.55]

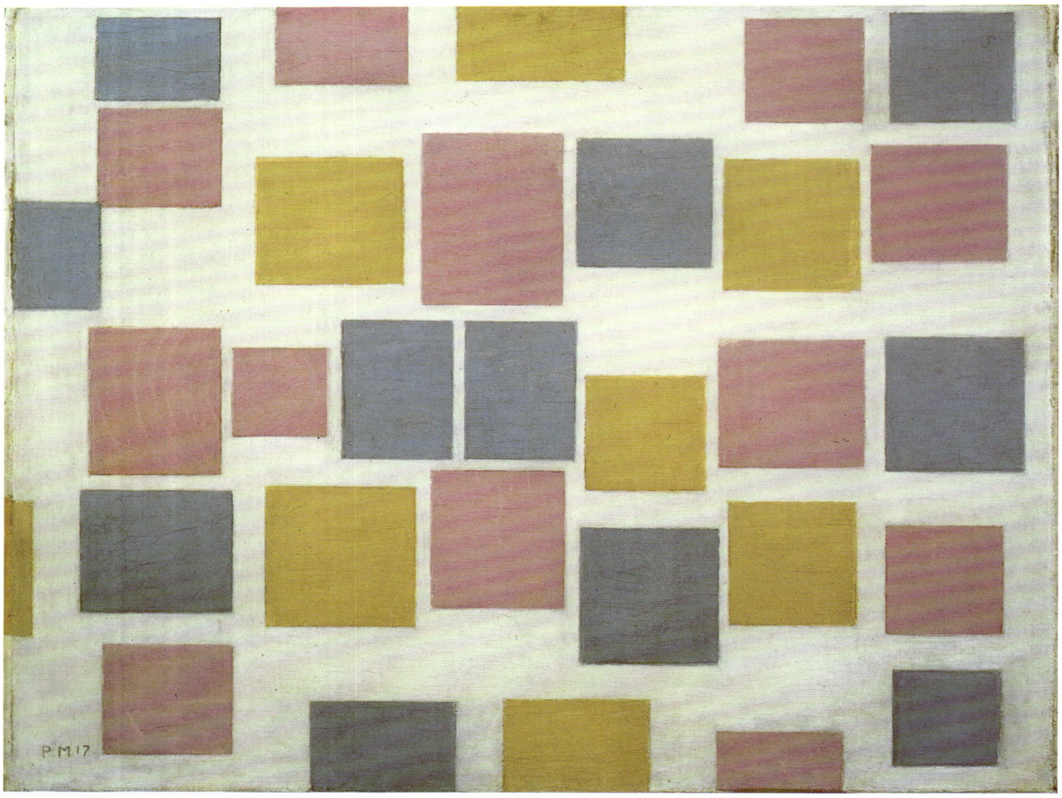

Composition with Colour Planes 3

1917 48 × 61cm [cat.56]

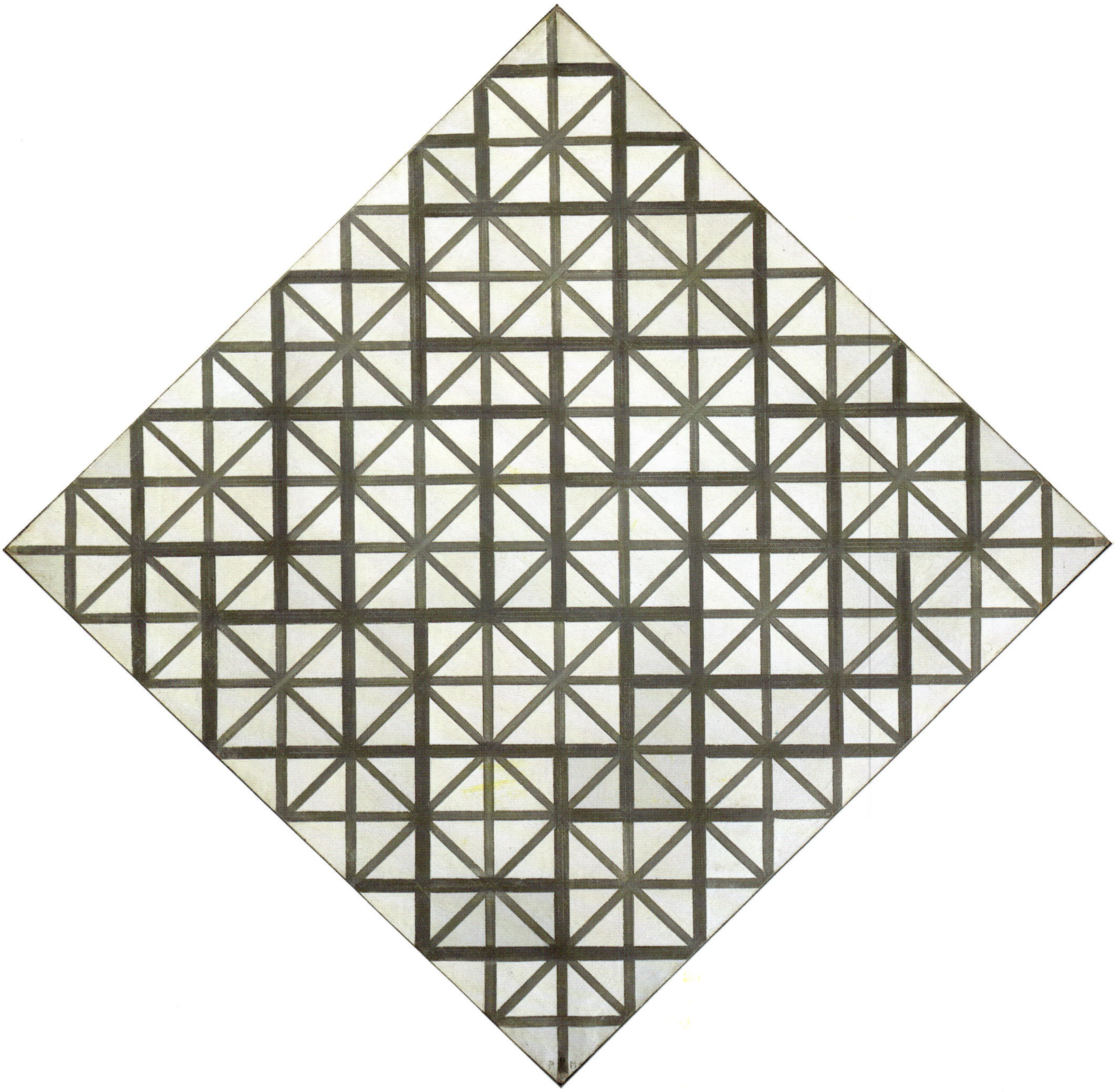

Composition with Grid (Lozenge)

1918 vertical axis 121cm [cat.57]

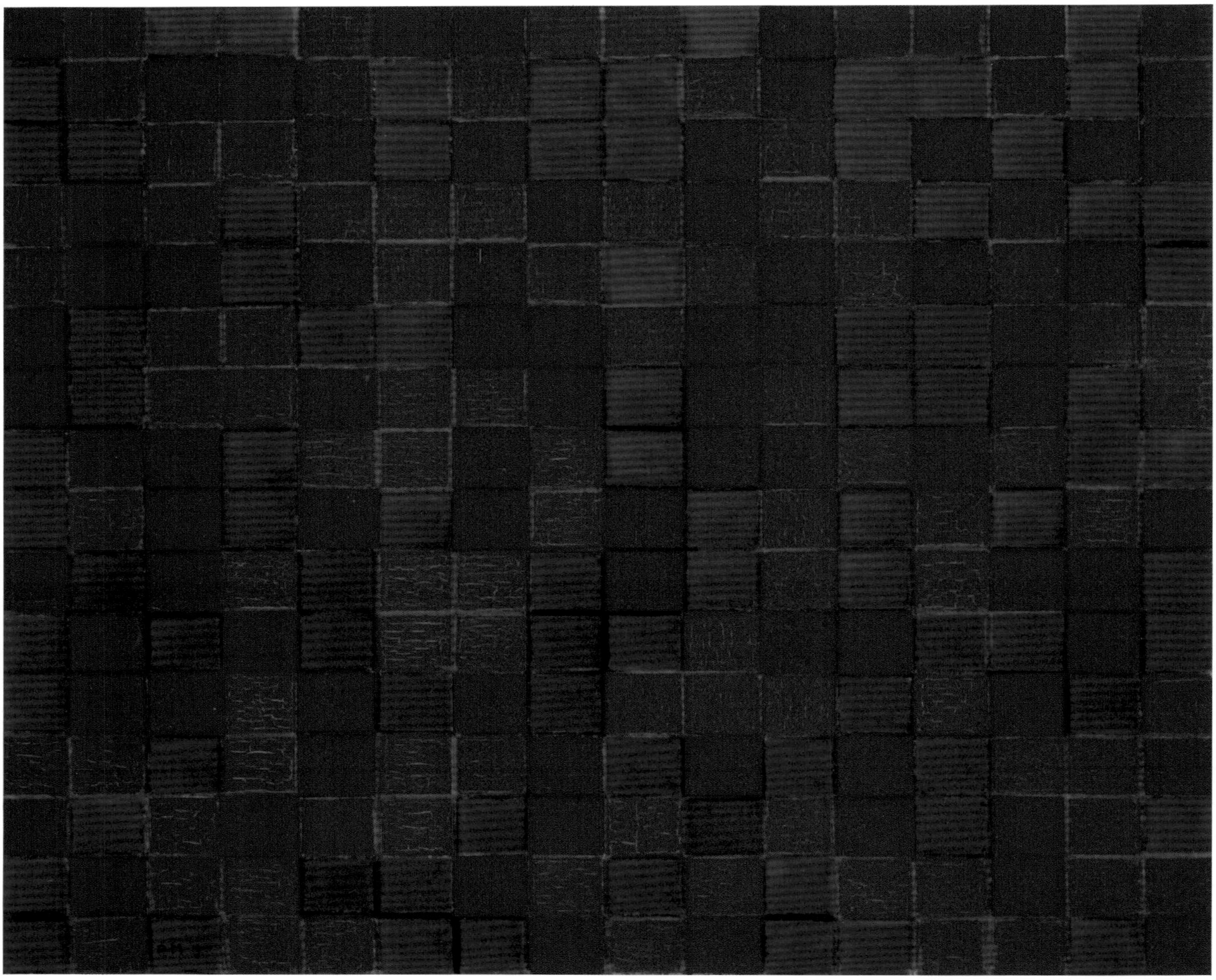

Composition Chequerboard: Dark Colours

1919 84 × 102cm [cat.58]

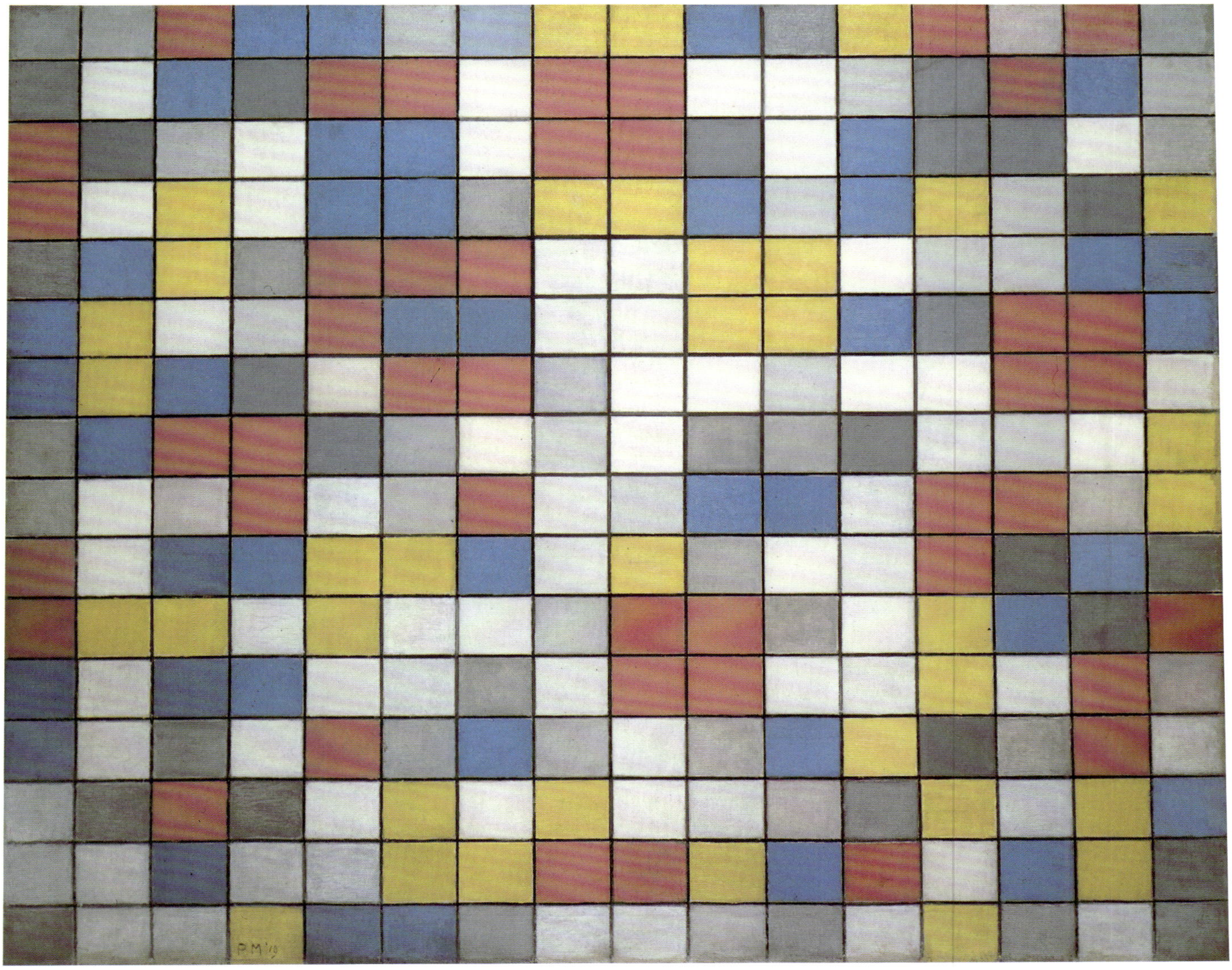

Composition Chequerboard: Light Colours

1919 86 × 106cm [cat.59]

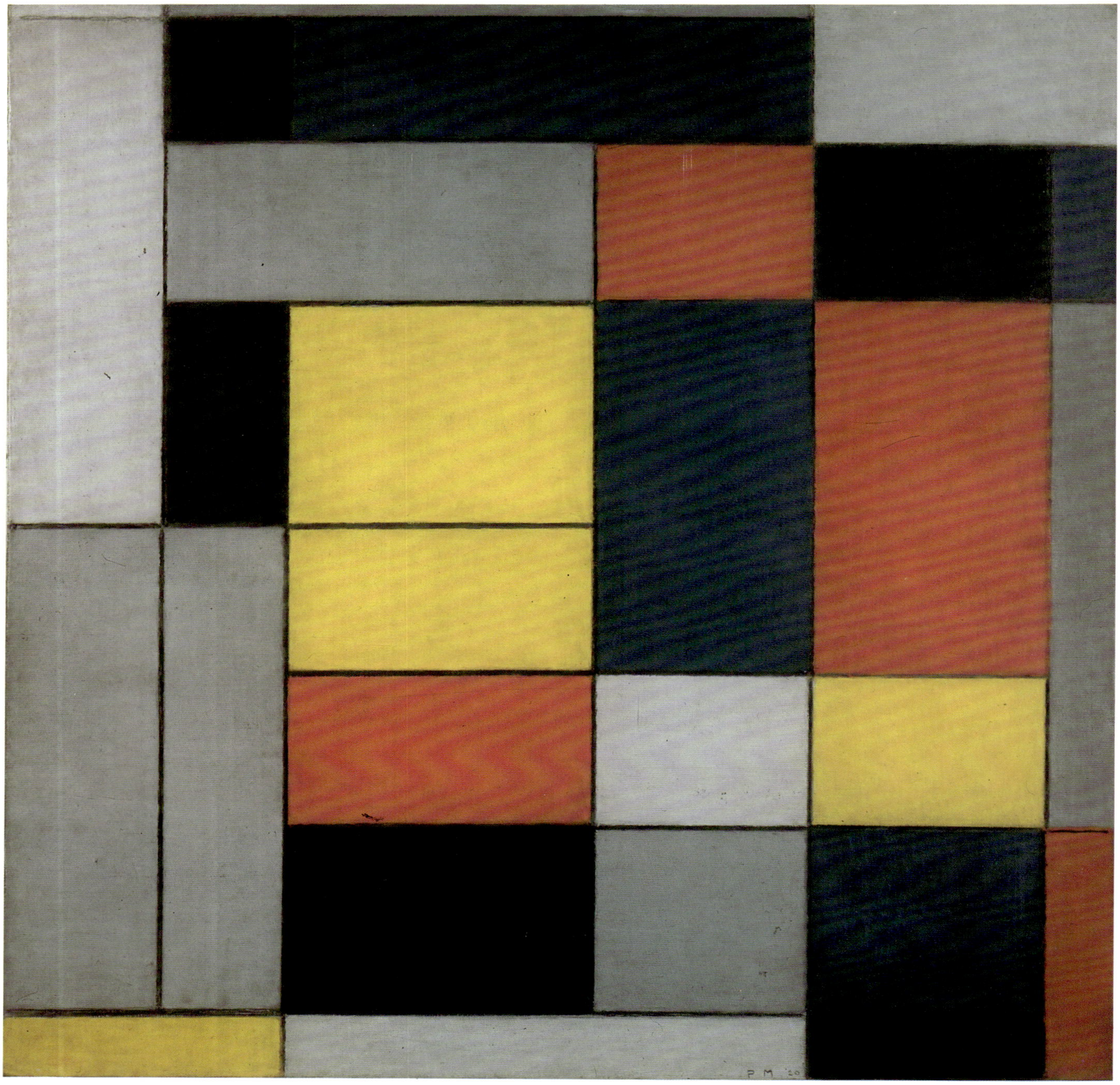

Composition with Grey, Red, Yellow and Blue

1920–c.1926 99.7 × 100.3cm [cat.60]

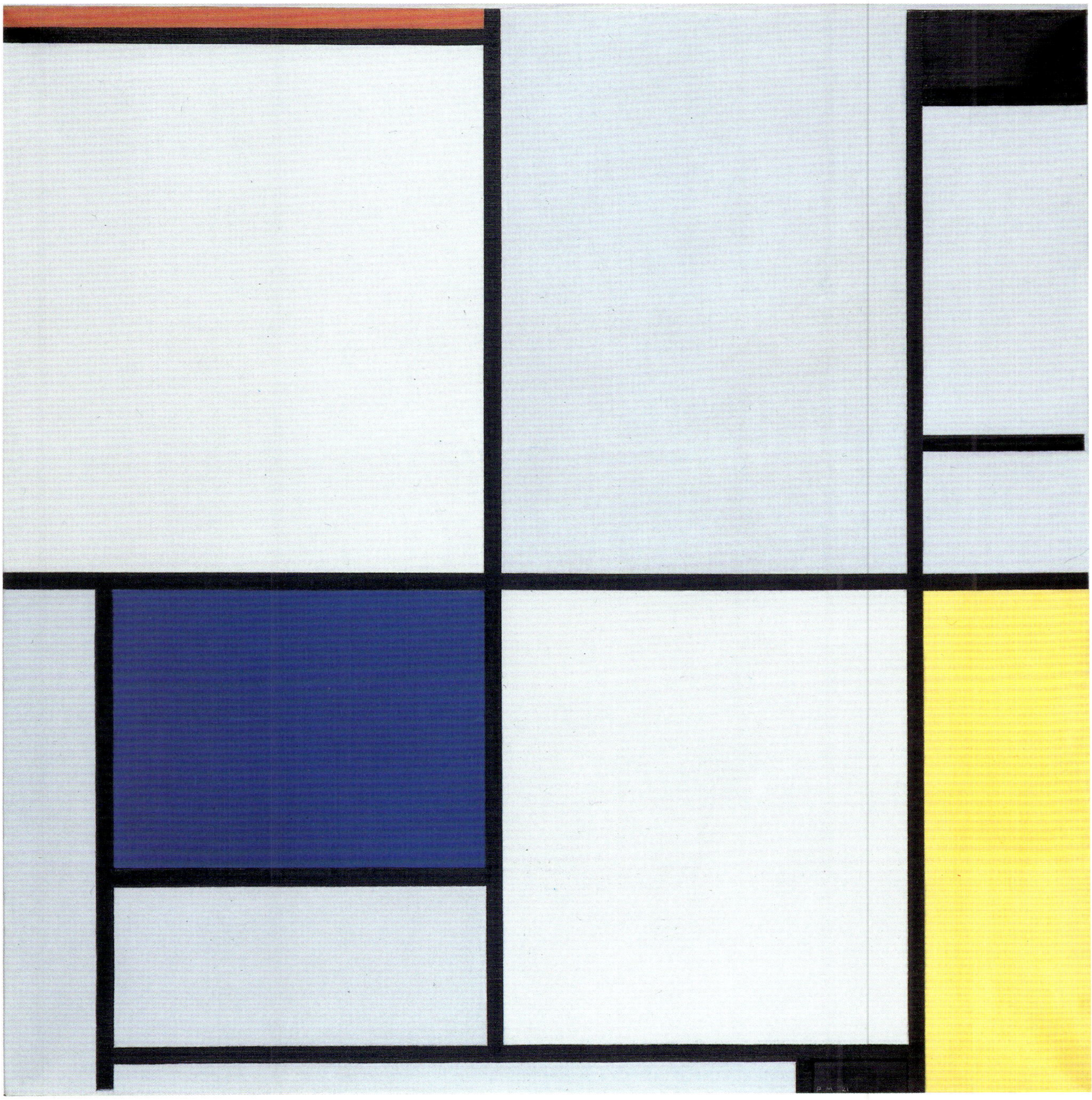

Composition with Red, Black, Blue and Yellow

1921 103 × 100cm [cat.61]

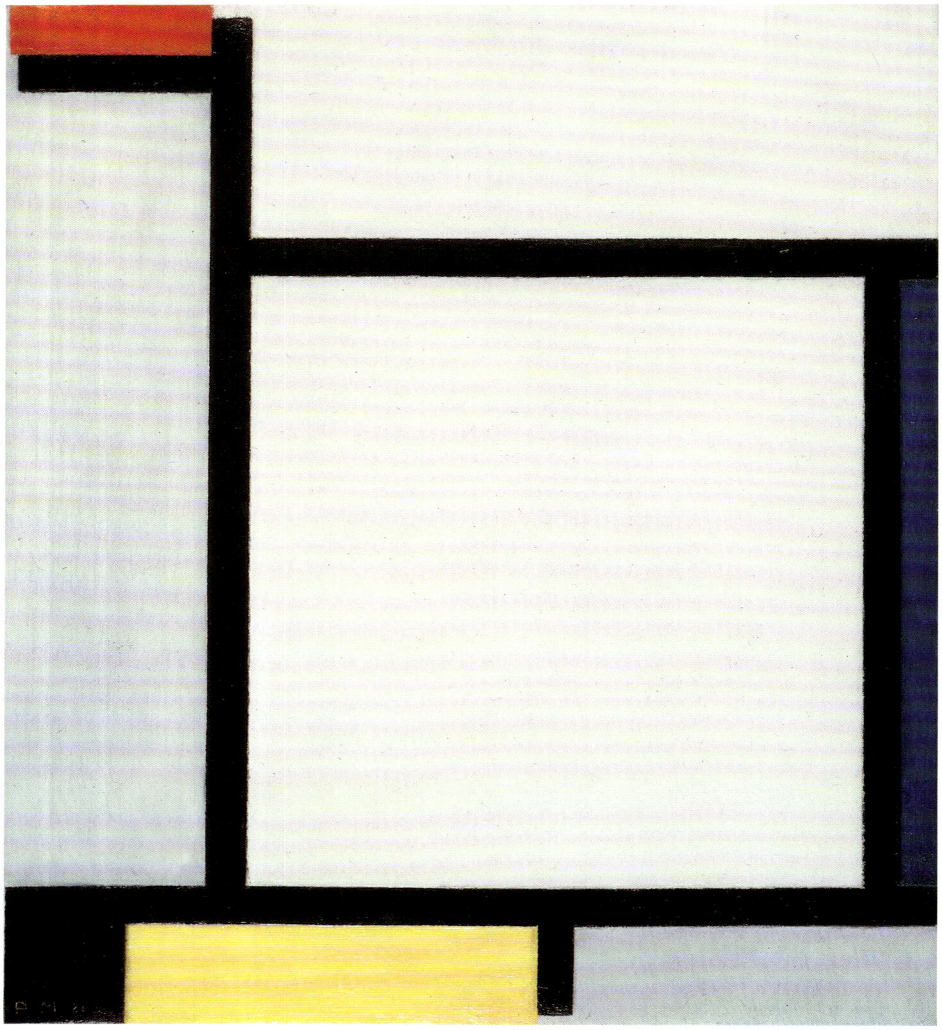

Composition with Red, Blue, Black, Yellow and Grey

1921 39.5 × 35cm [cat.62]

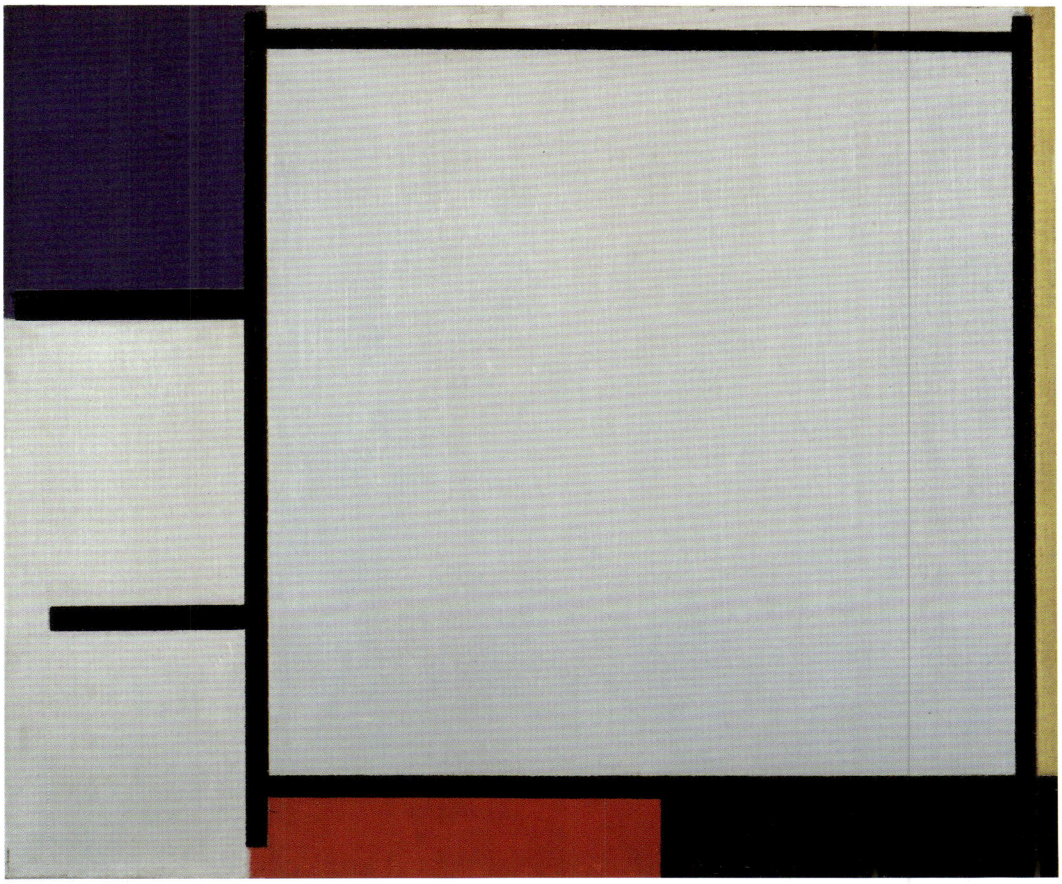

Composition with Blue, Yellow, Red, Black and Grey

1922 42 × 49cm [cat.63]

Composition with Yellow Lines

1933 vertical axis 113cm [cat.64]

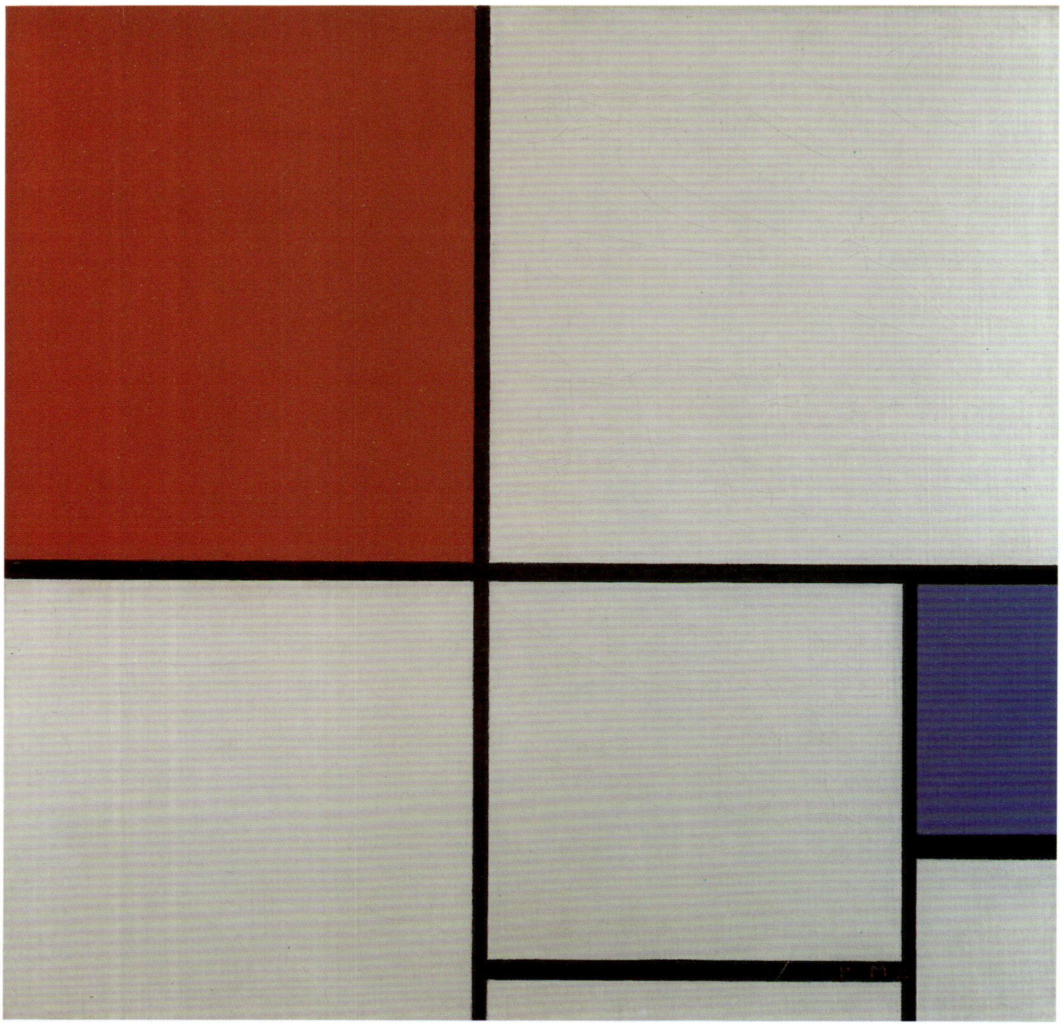

Composition A: Composition with Red and Blue

1932 54.9 × 54.9cm [cat.65]
not exhibited

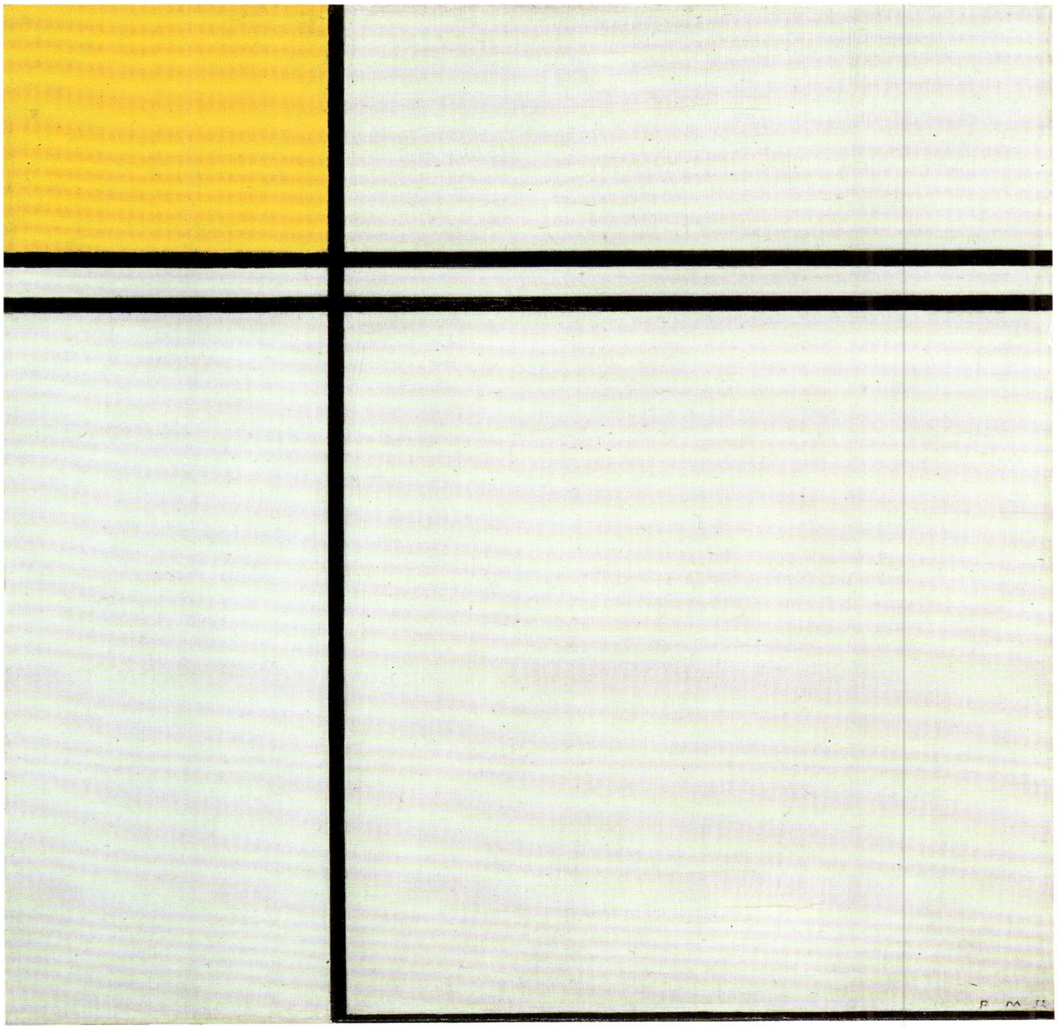

Composition with Yellow and Double Line

1932 45.3 × 45.3cm [cat.66]

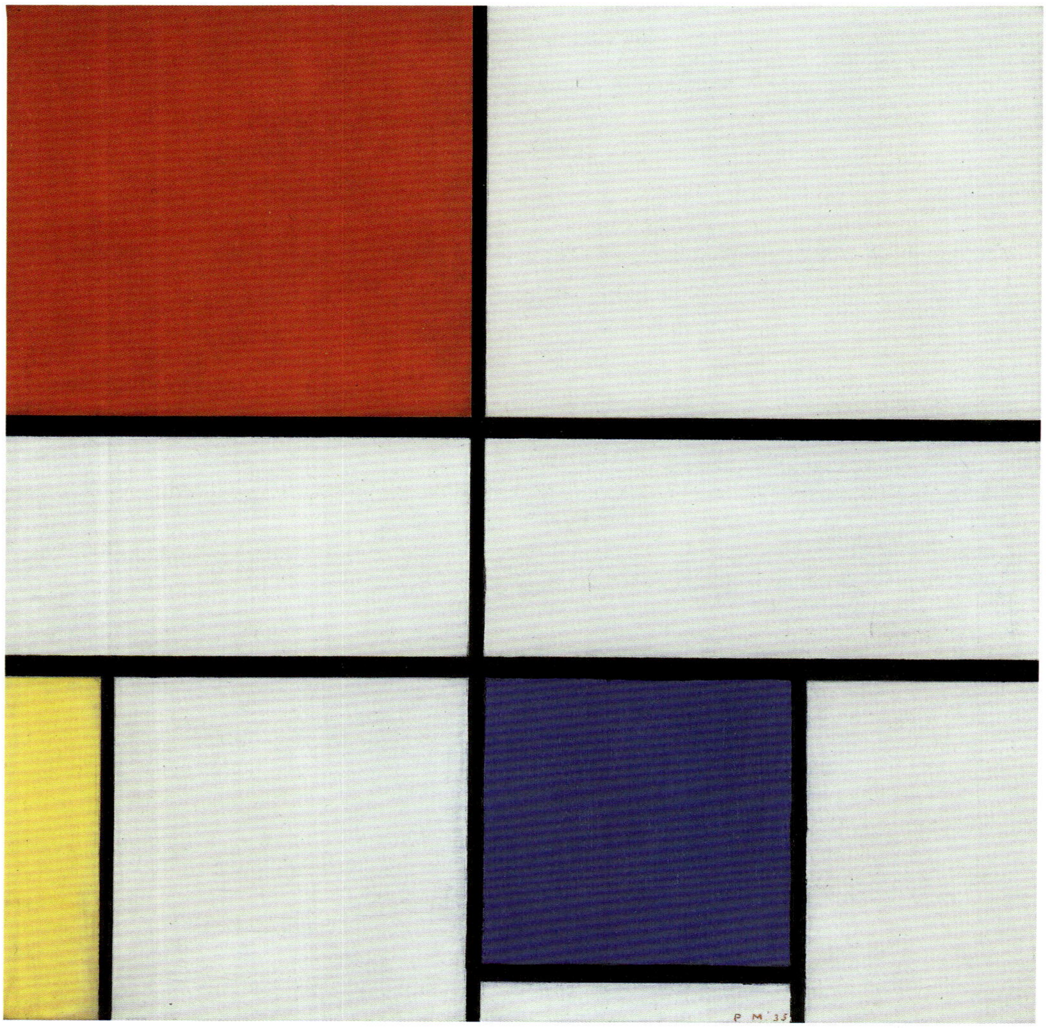

Composition with Red, Yellow and Blue

1935 56 × 55.2cm [cat.67]

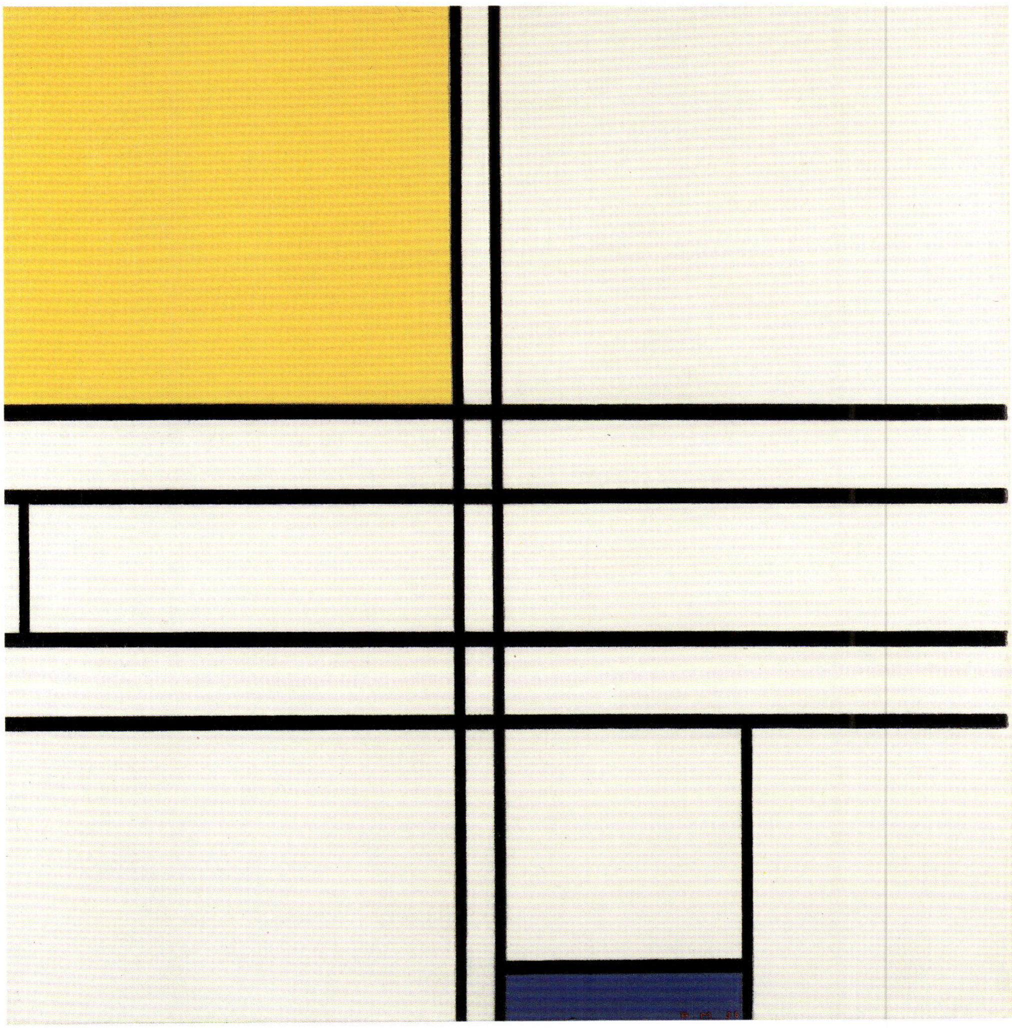

Composition C: Composition with Yellow and Blue

1936 72 × 69cm [cat.68]
not exhibited

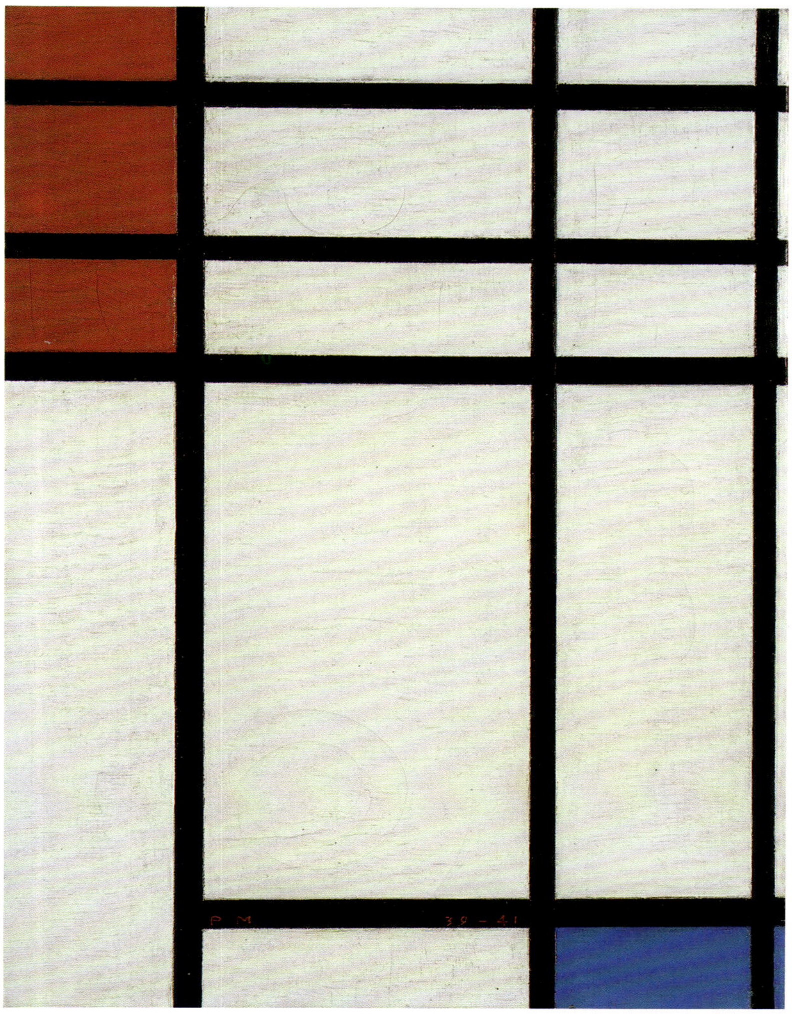

Composition of Red, Blue and White

1939 43.5 × 33cm [cat.69]

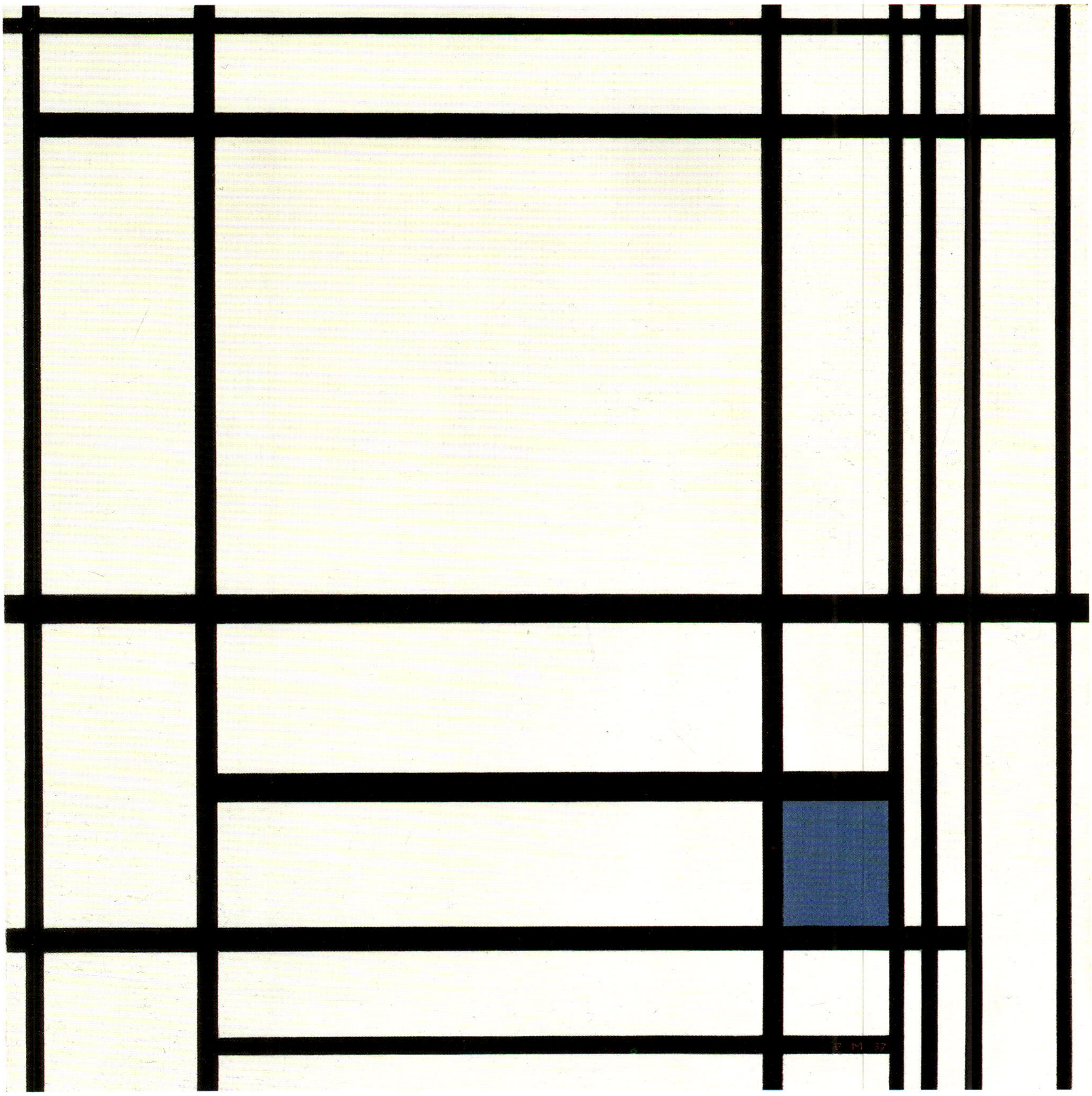

Composition of Lines and Colour III: Composition with Blue

1937 80 × 77cm [cat.70]

LIST OF EXHIBITED WORKS

Unless stated otherwise all the works are from the collection of the Haags Gemeentemuseum, The Hague.

Dimensions are given in centimetres followed by inches in brackets; height before width.

1 **Forest** 1898–1900
Watercolour and gouache on paper 45.5 × 57 (17⅞ × 22⅜)
Illustrated on p.37

2 **Country Road and Row of Houses** ?c.1898
Oil on paper 39 × 29.5 (15⅜ × 11⅝)
Illustrated on p.38

3 **Wax Candle Factory** 1900–1
Oil on canvas/card 35 × 48 (13¾ × 18⅞)
Illustrated on p.38

4 **Ditch near the Gein** 1901–2
Oil on canvas 23.5 × 37.5 (9¼ × 14¾)
Illustrated on p.39

5 **Ditch and Cows** 1901–2
Oil on canvas 20.5 × 38.5 (8 × 15⅛)
Illustrated on p.39

6 **Farm with Trees and Water** 1906
Chalk and pastel on paper 47.5 × 61.5 (18¾ × 24¼)
Illustrated on p.40

7 **Geinrust Farm in the Mist** 1906–7
Oil on canvas 32.5 × 42.5 (12¾ × 16¾)
Illustrated on p.41

8 **Solitary Tree** ?1907
Chalk on paper 14 × 19 (5½ × 7½)
Illustrated on p.42

9 **Evening on the Gein** 1906
Oil on canvas 65 × 86 (25⅝ × 33¾)
Illustrated on p.43

10 **Large Landscape** 1907
Oil on canvas 75 × 120 (29½ × 47¼)
Illustrated on p.45

11 **Sheepfold in the Evening** 1906
Charcoal, chalk and watercolour on paper 74 × 98 (29⅛ × 38½)
Illustrated on p.46

12 **Mill on the Gein** 1906–7
Oil on canvas 34.5 × 44.5 (13⅝ × 17½)
Illustrated on p.47

13 **Landscape with Cloud** 1907
Oil on canvas 36 × 49.5 (14⅛ × 19½)
Illustrated on p.47

14 **Trees on the Gein: Moonrise** 1907–8
Oil on canvas 79 × 92.5 (31⅛ × 36⅜)
Illustrated on p.48

15 **Red Cloud** 1907
Oil on canvas 64 × 75 (25⅛ × 29½)
Illustrated on p.49

16 **Woods near Oele** 1908
Oil on canvas 128 × 158 (50⅜ × 62⅛)
Illustrated on p.51

17 **Red Tree** 1908
Oil on canvas 70 × 99 (27½ × 39)
Illustrated on p.52

18 **Blue Tree** 1908–9
Tempera on card 75.5 × 99.5 (29¾ × 39⅛)
Illustrated on p.53

19 **Mill in Sunlight** 1908
Oil on canvas 114 × 87 (44⅞ × 30¼)
Illustrated on p.54

20 **Sea after Sunset** 1909
Oil on canvas 62.5 × 74.5 (24⅝ × 29¼)
Illustrated on p.55

21 **Sea after Sunset** 1909
Oil on canvas 41 × 76 (16⅛ × 29⅞)
Illustrated on p.56

22 **Lighthouse at Westkapelle** 1909
Oil on card 39 × 29.5 (15⅜ × 11⅝)
Illustrated on p.57

23 **Dune II** 1909
Oil on canvas 37.5 × 46.5 (14¾ × 18¼)
Illustrated on p.58

24 **Dune III** 1909
Oil on card 29.5 × 39 (11⅝ × 15⅜)
Illustrated on p.59

25 **Seascape** 1909
Oil on card 34.5 × 50.5 (13½ × 19⅞)
Illustrated on p.60

26 **Dune IV** 1909–10
Oil on card 33 × 46 (13 × 18⅛)
Illustrated on p.61

27 **Dune I** 1909
Oil on card 30 × 40 (11¾ × 15¾)
Illustrated on p.62

28 **Dune V** 1909–10
Oil on canvas 65.5 × 96 (25¾ × 37¾)
Illustrated on p.63

29 **Dying Chrysanthemum** 1908
Oil on canvas 84.5 × 54 (33¼ × 21¼)
Illustrated on p.64

30 **Mill at Domburg** 1909
Oil on card 76.5 × 63.5 (30⅛ × 25)
Illustrated on p.65

31 **Evolution** 1910–11
Oil on canvas, 3 sections 181.8 × 87.8, 187.1 × 90.6, 181.8 × 87.8 (71⅝ × 34½, 73⅝ × 35⅝, 71⅝ × 34½)
Illustrated on p.67

32 **Church at Domburg** 1910–11
Oil on canvas 114 × 75 (44⅞ × 29½)
Illustrated on p.68

33 **Red Mill** 1910–11
Oil on canvas 150 × 86 (59 × 29⅞)
Illustrated on p.69

34 **Sea** 1913–14
Pencil on paper 11.4 × 15.8 (4½ × 6¼)
Illustrated on p.70

35 **Sea** 1914
Pencil on paper 11.4 × 15.8 (4½ × 6¼)
Illustrated on p.70

36 **The Sea** 1912
Oil on canvas 82.5 × 92 (32½ × 36¼)
Private Collection, Switzerland
Illustrated on p.71

37 **Grey Tree** 1912
Oil on canvas 78.5 × 107.5 (30⅞ × 42¼)
Illustrated on p.72

38 **Flowering Appletree** 1912
Oil on canvas 78 × 106 (30⅞ × 42⅜)
Illustrated on p.73

39 **Studies of Trees II** 1913
Charcoal on paper 65.5 × 87.5 (25¾ × 34½)
Illustrated on p.74

40 **Study of Trees I** 1912
Chalk on paper 65 × 89 (25½ × 35)
Illustrated on p.75

41 **Forest** 1912
Chalk on paper 73 × 63 (28¾ × 24¾)
Illustrated on p.76

42 **Composition Trees II** 1912
Oil on canvas 98 × 65 (38½ × 25½)
Illustrated on p.77

43 **Tree (study)** 1913
Pencil on paper 13.4 × 17.8 (5¼ × 7)
Illustrated on p.78

44 **Tree (study)** 1913
Pencil on paper 17 × 12.3 (6¾ × 4⅞)
Illustrated on p.78

45 **Study of a Tree** 1913
Pencil on paper 12.4 × 17.8 (4⅞ × 7)
Trustees of the British Museum
Illustrated on p.78

46 **Tree** c.1913
Oil on canvas 100.3 × 67.3 (39½ × 26½)
Tate Gallery. Purchased 1977
Illustrated on p.79

47 **Composition in Oval** 1913
Charcoal on paper 85 × 70 (33½ × 27½)
Illustrated on p.80

48 **Composition III in Colour** 1913
Oil on canvas 95 × 80 (37⅜ × 31½)
Illustrated on p.81

49 **Composition 6** 1914
Oil on canvas 88 × 61 (34⅝ × 24)
Illustrated on p.82

50 **Composition in Oval with Colour Planes** 1914
Oil on canvas 113 × 84.5 (44½ × 33¼)
Illustrated on p.83

51 **Façade** 1912–14
Pencil on paper 15.8 × 11.4 (6¼ × 4½)
Illustrated on p.84

52 **Sketch for 'Blue Façade'** 1914
Pencil on paper 17.2 × 10.5 (6¾ × 4⅛)
Illustrated on p.84

53 **Church at Domburg** 1913–14
Pencil on paper 17.2 × 10.5 (6¾ × 4⅛)
Illustrated on p.84

54 **Church at Domburg** 1914
Ink on paper 63 × 50 (24¾ × 19¾)
Illustrated on p.85

55 **Sea, Pier and Ocean** 1914
Charcoal on paper 51 × 63 (20 × 24¾)
Illustrated on p.87

56 **Composition with Colour Planes 3** 1917
Oil on canvas 48 × 61 (18⅞ × 24)
Illustrated on p.88

57 **Composition with Grid (Lozenge)** 1918
Oil on canvas, vertical axis 121 (47⅝)
Illustrated on p.89

58 **Composition Chequerboard: Dark Colours** 1919
Oil on canvas 84 × 102 (33 × 40⅛)
Illustrated on p.90

59 **Composition Chequerboard: Light Colours** 1919
Oil on canvas 86 × 106 (33⅞ × 41¾)
Illustrated on p.91

60 **Composition with Grey, Red, Yellow and Blue** 1920–c.1926
Oil on canvas 99.7 × 100.3 (39¼ × 39½)
Tate Gallery. Purchased 1967
Illustrated on p.92

61 **Composition with Red, Black, Blue and Yellow** 1921
Oil on canvas 103 × 100 (40⅝ × 39⅜)
Illustrated on p.93

62 **Composition with Red, Blue, Black, Yellow and Grey** 1921
Oil on canvas 39.5 × 35 (15½ × 13⅞)
Illustrated on p.94

63 **Composition with Blue, Yellow, Red, Black and Grey** 1922
Oil on canvas 42 × 49 (16½ × 19¼)
Stedelijk Museum, Amsterdam
Illustrated on p.95

64 **Composition with Yellow Lines** 1933
Oil on canvas, vertical axis 113 (44½)
Illustrated on p.97

not exhibited
65 **Composition A: Composition with Red and Blue** 1932
Oil on canvas 54.9 × 54.9 (21⅝ × 21⅝)
Kunstmuseum Winterthur, Bequest of Clara and Emil Friedrich-Jezler Kunstverein
Illustrated on p.98

66 **Composition with Yellow and Double Line** 1932
Oil on canvas 45.3 × 45.3 (17⅞ × 17⅞)
The Scottish National Gallery of Modern Art, Edinburgh
Illustrated on p.99

67 **Composition with Red, Yellow and Blue** 1935
Oil on canvas 56 × 55.2 (22 × 21⅝)
Private Collection
Illustrated on p.100

not exhibited
68 **Composition C: Composition with Yellow and Blue** 1936
Oil on canvas 72 × 69 (28⅜ × 27⅛)
Private Collection
Illustrated on p.101

69 **Composition of Red, Blue and White** 1939
Oil on canvas 43.5 × 33 (17⅛ × 13)
Private Collection
Illustrated on p.102

70 **Composition of Lines and Colour III: Composition with Blue** 1937
Oil on canvas 80 × 77 (31½ × 30¼)
Illustrated on p.103

CHRONOLOGY

1872
Piet Mondrian born in Amersfoort, 7 March.

1880
Moves to Winterswijk where his father is appointed headmaster of the Christian school.

1886
Leaves school and studies drawing and painting.

1889
Passes 'Lower Certificate' and teaches at his father's school.

1892
Moves to Amsterdam and enters the Rijksacademie.

1893
First exhibition at Kunstliefde in Utrecht.

1895
Leaves the Rijksacademie. Undertakes a great deal of copying.

1896
Enters evening drawing class at the Rijksacademie.

1897
Becomes member of St Lucas, the artists' association for students at the Rijksacademie.

1898
Undertakes many copies and commissions. Works in the summers in Winterswijk and starts to exhibit more frequently.

1903
Works in Brabant. Around this time he is acquainted with the work of Charles Daubigny through the Collection Mesdag in The Hague.

1904
Moves to Uden in Brabant where he applies himself to painting scenes of agricultural life. Becomes member of the board of the St Lucas association. Makes trips with artist friends to the landscape south of Amsterdam, along the Gein and the Amstel.

1905
Exhibition of mostly early work by Vincent van Gogh in the Stedelijk Museum. Mondrian shows a great deal, but sells little.

1906
Wins the Willink van Collen prize. Achieves a reputation with evening landscapes, on which he works mainly in Oele and Twente.

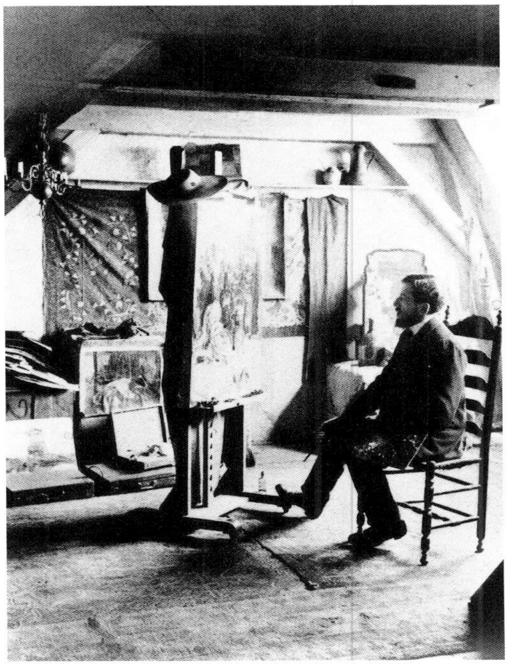

Mondrian in his studio, Amsterdam 1905

1908
Towards the end of summer visits the fashionable seaside resort of Domburg in Zeeland where a circle of avant-garde artists, grouped around Jan Toorop and collector Marie Tak van Poortvliet, were especially interested in Divisionism and other new modes of expression. Exhibition of the work done in France by Vincent van Gogh at Kunsthandel C.M. van Gogh in Amsterdam.

1909
Survey exhibition in the Stedelijk Museum of work by Cornelis Spoor, Piet Mondrian and Jan Sluyters.

1910
Elected to the Board of the recently established Moderne Kunst Kring in which all progressive Dutch artists are united. Breaks with St Lucas and stops showing at Arti.

1911
Exhibits work in Nantes and Paris where he goes to prepare the first exhibition of the Moderne Kunst Kring. Becomes acquainted with the work of Picasso and Le Fauconnier. Moves to Paris. Almost marries Greta Heijboek, but changes his mind.

1912–14
Commissioned by Marie Tak van Poortvliet to make a copy of Enquerrand Quarton's *Avignon Pietà* in the Louvre. Sends work to the Sonderbund Ausstellung in Cologne and the exhibition *Toorop, Schelfhout and the Dutch* at the Salon der neuen Kunst in Munich, and participates in the *Erster Deutscher Herbstsalon* at Galerie Der Sturm in Berlin where he uses neutral titles for his works for the first time. Works in Paris and only returns to the Netherlands to visit family and friends, and for a holiday at Domburg. Broadens his selection of motifs from trees to blind façades.

1914
Gets to know H.P. Bremmer, adviser to Mrs Kröller-Müller, an art collector interested in Mondrian's work. Through Bremmer he secures an exhibition at Walrecht in The Hague where he shows Cubist works. Exhibits in Zurich and Prague. Returns to the Netherlands to visit his father who has been taken ill, and is forced by the outbreak of the First World War to remain in the Netherlands. Attempts to publish articles about his intentions. Works in Domburg on a series of drawings using the motifs of the Domburg church tower and the sea.

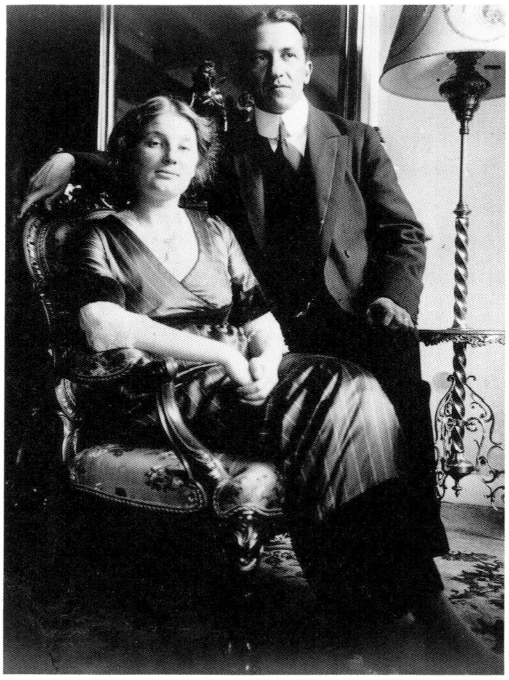

Mondrian and Greta Heijbroek, 1911

1915

Finds shelter in the village of Laren where many artists live cheaply. Exhibits in Rotterdam and Amsterdam. Gets acquainted with Sal Slijper who starts to collect his work with an emphasis on the early paintings. Gets to know Theo van Doesburg, artist and critic, who writes admiringly about one of the abstract compositions shown in Amsterdam.

1916

Shows at the second exhibition of the Hollandsche Kunstenaarskring. Works hard on the text about his ideas on art: 'all art is good; one's own is merely the result of what has been done, and yet points toward the spirit of the coming age.' Meets Bart van der Leck. Makes copies for a living.

1917

Follows van Doesburg's suggestion to submit a recently finished manuscript about 'De Nieuwe Beelding in de Schilderkunst' (The New Plastic in Painting) for publication in a new magazine. At the beginning of November the first issue of the magazine, *De Stijl* (The Style), appears.

1918

Works further on his paintings, which are becoming increasingly regular, and in which every representational reference seems to have disappeared. Aims to express relationships rather than objects in his works. Experiments with the possibilities of regular subdivision.

1919

Writes a dialogue and a trialogue for *De Stijl* to express his intentions in an accessible way. Packs up the works from 1914 onwards that are still in his possession, sells all the earlier, naturalistic paintings to Sal Slijper and leaves for Paris where he starts work on his first Neo-plastic composition, *Composition A* (fig.3 on p.17). Experiments in his studio with coloured pieces of paper, which he puts on the wall. Is pleased with the effect on his painting.

1920

Writes about the Dada movement in Paris. Produces thirty-eight Neo-plastic paintings. Differs in opinion with Leopold Survage and Georges Vantongerloo about the harmony of colours and concludes that 'a balanced relation can exist with discords'. Writes a brochure on Neo-plasticism to promote his ideas in France.

1921

His father dies. Sells work through artist friends in the Netherlands. Exhibits at Léonce Rosenberg's Galerie de 'L'Effort Moderne'. Writes about Futurism and about the new harmony. Moves to the rue de Départ, to the studio where he lived until 1914. Arranges it according to the rules of Neo-plasticism. Friends who visit talk about the radical layout of the interior and journalists write about it in Dutch newspapers. This makes him known to a larger public.

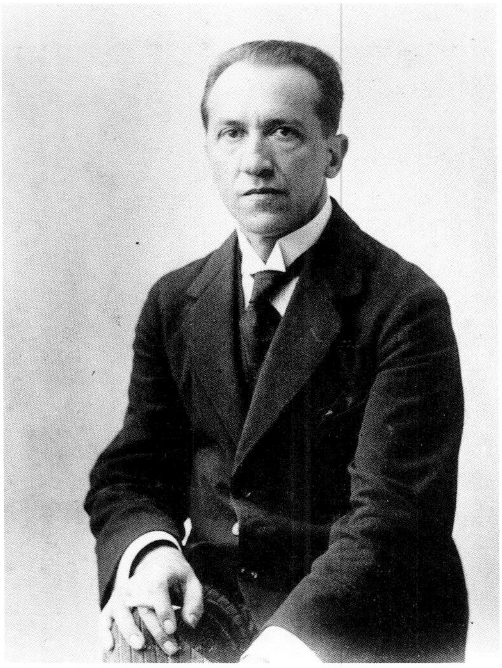

Piet Mondrian, c.1919

1922
Writes again about music. Makes watercolours of flowers for a living and from time to time derives pleasure from it. Is honoured on the initiative of Sal Slijper with a retrospective exhibition at the eighth annual show of the Hollandsche Kunstenaarskring. Writes about Neo-plasticism in architecture and about the need to use the principles in a non-decorative manner that does justice to the form.

1923
Spends more time on paintings and watercolours of still lifes with flowers. Participates in the Grosse Berliner Kunstausstellung. Moholy-Nagy reviews in *Der Sturm* Mondrian's articles on Neo-plasticism and music. Works more on articles and less on new paintings.

1924
Complies with an invitation to send a contribution to the Bauhausbücher. Herman Hana writes an elaborate review for *Wil en Weg* in which he tackles the early and the late work as well as the relationship between them. Comes into contact with El Lissitzky through Sophie Küppers. Sells work to the Provinzialmuseum in Hanover. Last contributions to *De Stijl*. Paints his atelier once more.

1925
Ends his contact with van Doesburg and works on new paintings, especially in diamond shapes, a form of composition which had concerned him in earlier works. Attends the debut of Josephine Baker in the Revue Nègre. Paints the studio with Vantongerloo. Receives ever more visitors to the studio who are interested in purchasing works. First painting sold to a French collector.

1926
Shows at Kunsthandlung Kühl und Kühn in Dresden and with Lissitzky at Galerie Hans Goltz in Munich. Makes more contacts with artists and collectors from Germany, Switzerland and the United States and says he'll never go back to the Netherlands if the Charleston is banned there. Publishes in the magazines *Vouloir*, *Cahiers d'Art* and *i10*.

1927
Works hard on new paintings. Writes about 'Jazz and Neo-plasticism', describing the closed musical form as an exponent of the old, the open rhythm as an exponent of the new. Changes the arrangement of his studio once more. Works on a book about 'art, life and society'.

1928
Participates in the exhibition *A.S.B. Architectuur, Schilderkunst, Beeldhouwkunst* in the Stedelijk Museum in Amsterdam with an important group of young artists, headed by Charley Toorop. Is part of the exhibit for the 16th Venice Biennial. A visit by Mart Stam and El Lissitzky provokes an absorption in the recent developments in architecture. Changes his studio.

1929
Renews contact with van Doesburg. Sells paintings to Katherine Dreier in New York. Participates in exhibitions of abstract art in Zurich and Munich.

1930
Writes a short text under the title 'Vouloir Construire' for *Cercle et Carré*. Meets Walter Gropius. Sells work to Hilla Rebay, Henry Russell-Hitchcock and again to Dreier. Tells Sal Slijper that he has no more time for flowers.

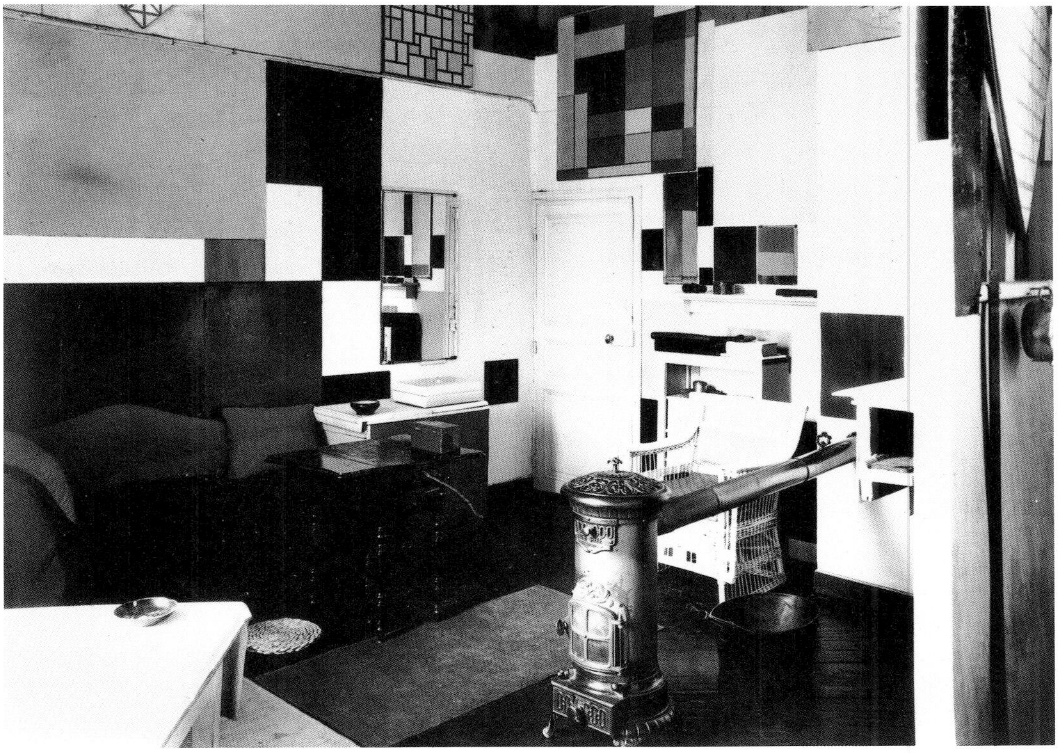

Mondrian's studio, 26 rue du Départ, Paris 1926

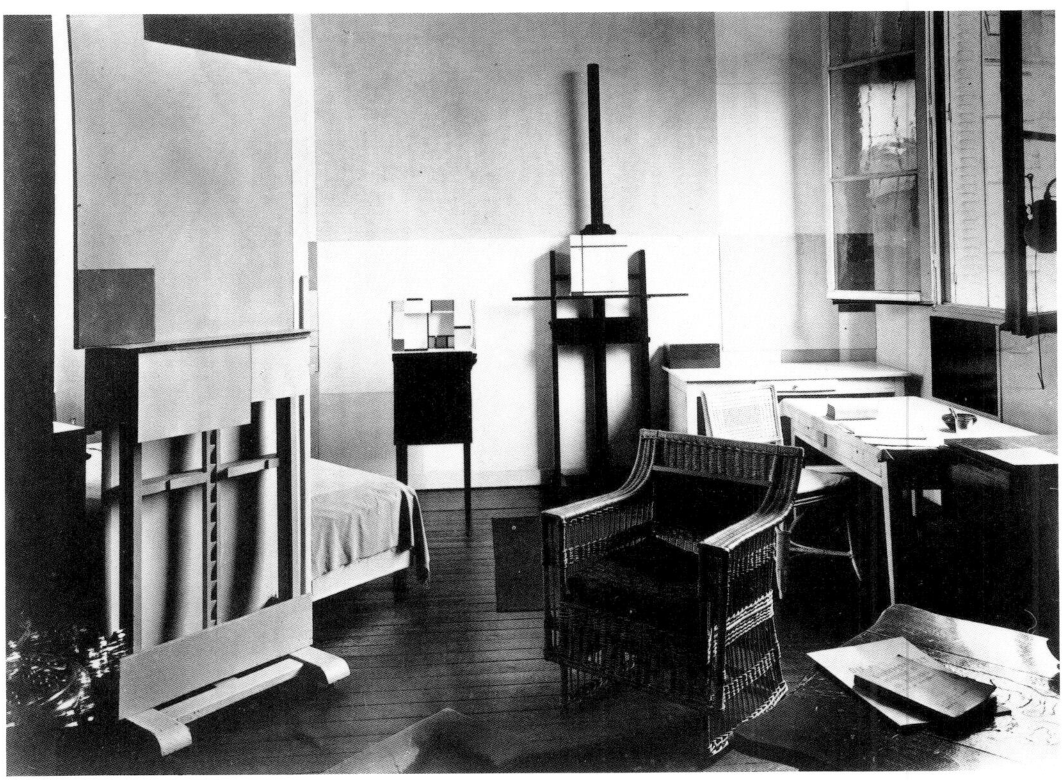

Mondrian's studio, Paris 1926

1931
Becomes member of Abstraction-Création, in which an international group of abstract artists combine forces. Sells a reasonable number of works through shows. Finishes his book *L'Art et la Vie: L'Art Nouveau – la Vie Nouvelle (La Culture des Rapports Pures)* in which he tries to explain a great number of diverse phenomena with the help of his theory. Makes paintings in which colour gradually vanishes and white planes and black lines of differing width dominate.

1932
Experiments with breaking through the closed structure of the black line by repeating it. This device becomes known as the double line. On the occasion of his sixtieth birthday a group of Dutch friends commissions a painting, which they want to offer to a Dutch museum.

1933
Stimulated by sale results, he works hard on canvases in which the double line dominates. Finishes the painting bought by his friends a year earlier. *Composition with Yellow Lines* (cat.64) is offered to the Haags Gemeentemuseum because the Stedelijk Museum has refused it.

1934
Through Abstraction-Création he makes the acquaintance of Barbara Hepworth, Ben and Winifred Nicholson. Maintains intense contact, especially with the latter. Works on a series of paintings, which he finishes in 1935, for exhibition in the United States. First hears the music of Louis Armstrong. Writes an article for *Axis* which is translated into English by Winifred Nicholson but is refused.

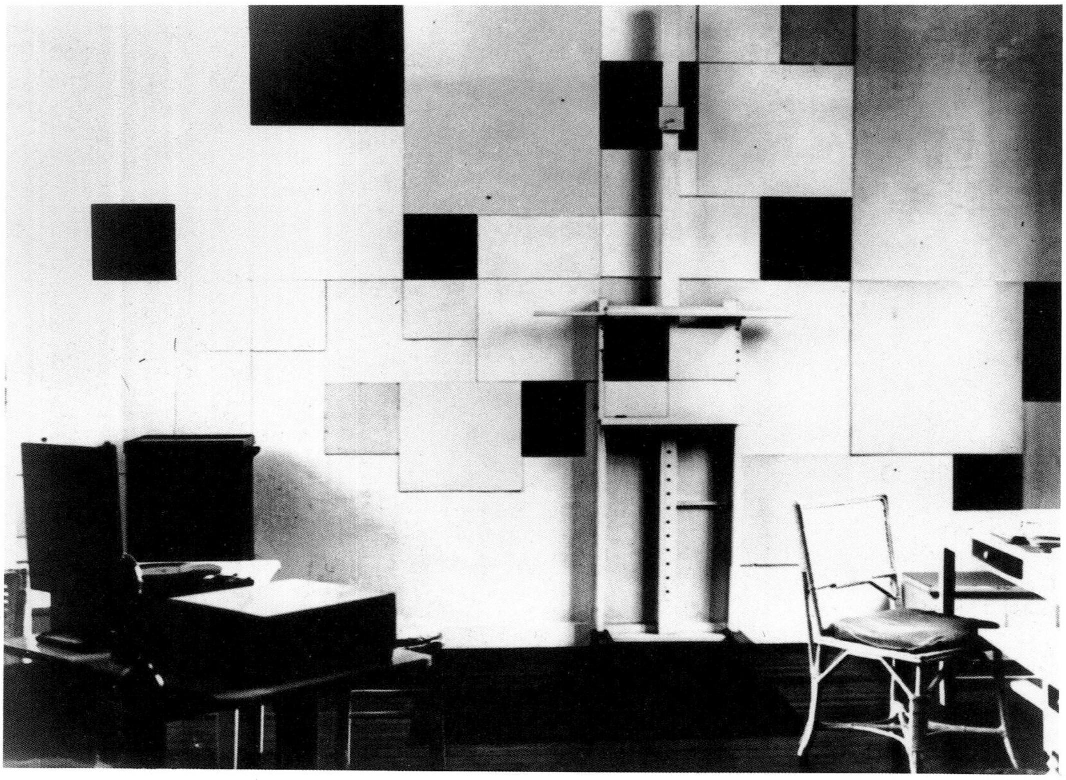

Mondrian's studio, Paris *c.*1930

1935
Unable to work because of rheumatic pains. Falls seriously ill and can resume painting only towards the end of the year.

1936
Shows in the exhibition *Abstract & Concrete* organised by *Axis* in Oxford. It travels to Liverpool, London and Cambridge. Comes into contact with artists and collectors in Great Britain and sells work. Moves from his studio in the rue de Départ to the boulevard Raspail. Experiments with colour planes attached to the wall.

1937
Works on paintings in which a dense, rhythmic network of black lines is contrasted with the sparing use of colours. Gets more and more attention from international art criticism. Finds his work declared degenerate by its inclusion in the show *Entartete Kunst* with which Germany manifests its new culture policy.

1938
Makes preparations to leave France for England. Travels to London where he has friends. Moves into a studio which he arranges simply and has painted white. Works on new paintings.

1939
Does little work because of the war threat. Shows in London, New York and Paris.

1940
The outbreak of war renders him unable to work. Gets a visa for the United States. Leaves England on 21 September after the strike of a V1-rocket close to his studio. Reaches New York after two weeks on deck in a convoy. Experiences Boogie Woogie and arranges a new studio. Starts to work on new paintings.

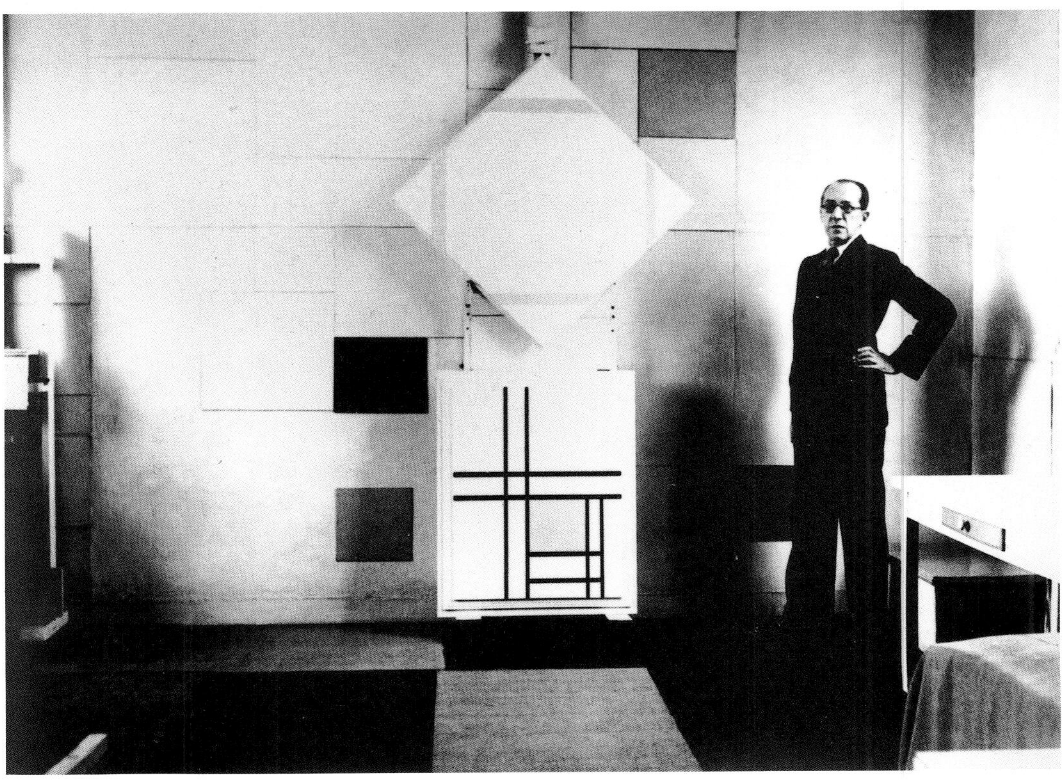

Mondrian in his studio, Paris 1933

1941–2

Plunges into the New York cultural milieu and makes new paintings for the first solo exhibition of his life, in a New York gallery. Changes the paintings he had brought from England by adding small colour planes, no longer limited by a black line.

1943

Makes new paintings and, stimulated by their success, moves to a larger apartment in the centre of the city. Works on paintings in which the colour is independent of black lines.

1944

Dies on 31 January.

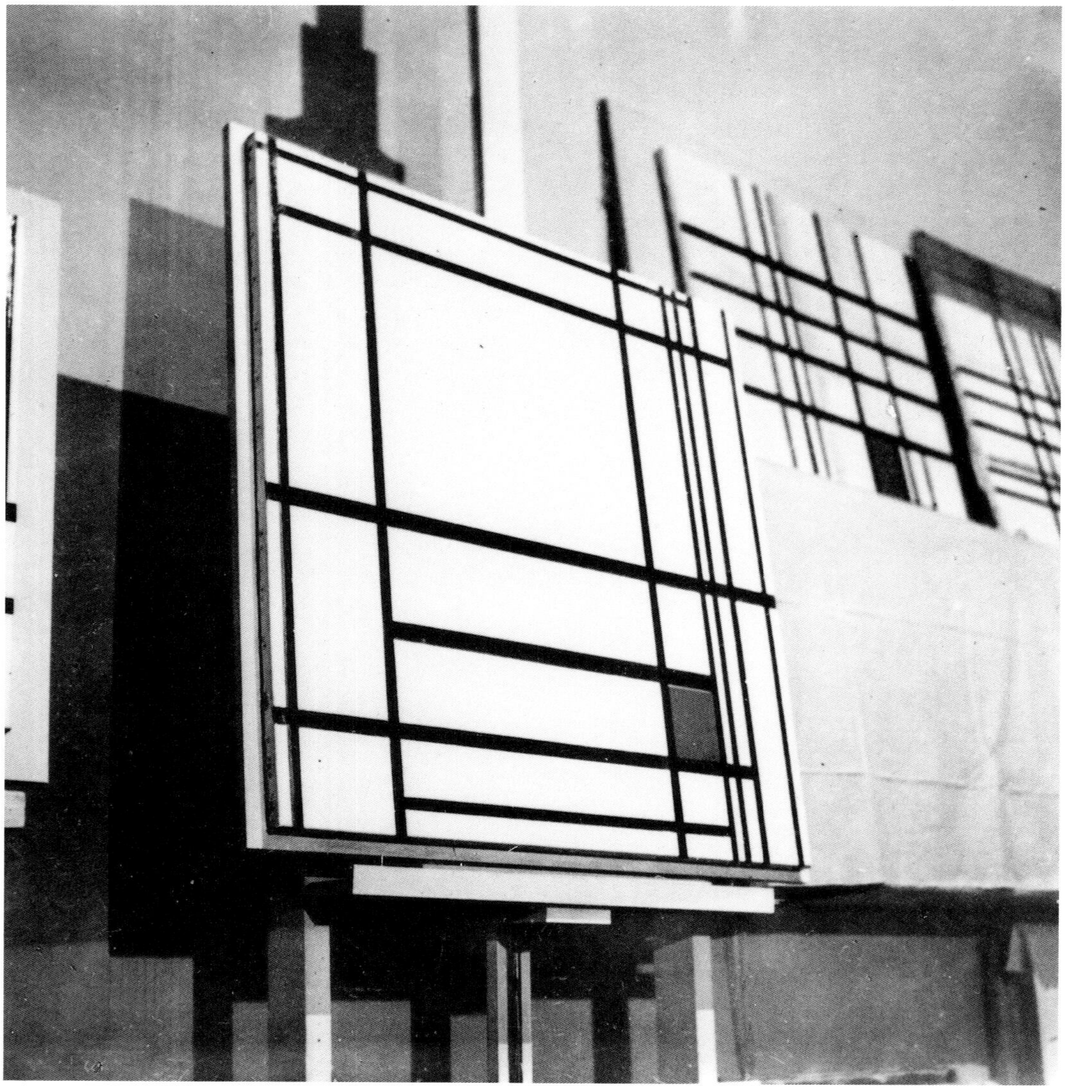

Mondrian's studio at boulevard Raspail, Paris 1937, with *Composition of Lines and Colour, III: Composition with Blue* (cat.70) on the easel

SELECTED EXHIBITIONS

Piet Mondrian. The Museum of Modern Art, New York, 21 March–13 May 1945.

Piet Mondriaan herdenkingstentoonstelling. Stedelijk Museum, Amsterdam, 6 November–16 December 1946.

Gedächtnis-Ausstellung Piet Mondrian. Kunsthalle, Basle, 6 February–2 March 1947.

Mondriaan. Haags Gemeentemuseum, The Hague, 10 February–12 April 1955; Kunsthaus, Zurich, 22 May–July 1955; 5 August–11 September 1955.

Piet Mondrian: The Earlier Years. The Solomon R. Guggenheim Museum, New York, 10 December–26 January 1958; The San Francisco Museum of Art, 6–23 February 1958.

Piet Mondrian: Centennial Exhibition. The Solomon R. Guggenheim Museum, New York, 8 October–12 December 1971.

Mondrian: The Diamond Compositions. National Gallery of Art, Washington, 15 July–16 September 1979.

Mondrian: Zeichnungen, Aquarelle, New Yorker Bilder | Teekeningen, aquarellen, New Yorkse schilderijen | Drawings, Watercolours, New York Paintings. Staatsgalerie, Stuttgart, 6 December 1980–15 February 1981; Haags Gemeentemuseum, The Hague, 20 March–31 May 1981; The Baltimore Museum of Art, 12 July–20 September 1981.

Mondrian in the Sidney Janis Family Collections, New York. Haags Gemeentemuseum, The Hague, 19 February–29 May 1988.

Piet Mondrian 1872–1944. Haags Gemeentemuseum, The Hague, 18 December 1994–30 April 1995; National Gallery of Art Washington, 11 June–4 September 1995; The Museum of Modern Art, New York, 1 October 1995–23 January 1996.

BIBLIOGRAPHY

Art of this Century. Objects–Drawings–Photographs–Paintings–Sculpture–Collages 1910 to 1942, ed. Peggy Guggenheim, New York 1942.

Barr, Jr., Alfred H., *Cubism and Abstract Art*, exh. cat., The Museum of Modern Art, New York 1936.

Barr, Jr., Alfred H., 'De Stijl,' preface by Philip C. Johnson, *The Museum of Modern Art Bulletin* vol.20, Winter 1952, pp.5–13.

Blok, Cor, *Piet Mondriaan. Een catalogus van zijn werk in Nederlands openbaar bezit*, Amsterdam, 1974.

Blotkamp, Carel, 'Mondrian's First Diamond Compositions,' *Artforum*, vol.18, December 1979, pp.33–9.

Blotkamp, Carel, *Mondrian: The Art of Destruction*, London 1994.

Bois, Yve-Alain, 'Du project au procès' in *L'Atelier de Mondrian*, ed. Yve-Alain Bois, Paris, 1982, pp.26–43.

Bois, Yve-Alain, 'Piet Mondrian, *New York City*' in *Paintings as Model*, Cambridge, Mass. and London 1990, pp.157–83.

Bremmer, H.P., *Catalogus van de schilderijen verzameling van mevrouw H. Kröller-Müller*, The Hague, 1917, 1921, 1925.

Carmean, Jr., E.A., *Mondrian: The Diamond Compositions*, exh. cat., National Gallery of Art, Washington 1979.

Champa, Kermit Swiller, *Mondrian Studies*, Chicago and London 1985.

Circle: International Survey of Constructive Art, ed. J.L. Martin, Ben Nicholson and N. Gabo, London 1937.

Elgar, Frank, *Mondrian*, New York, Washington and London 1968.

Golding, John, *Cubism: A History and an Analysis, 1907–1914*, London 1959.

Green, Christopher, *Léger and the Avant-Garde*, New Haven and London 1976.

Harrison, Charles, 'Mondrian in London: Reminiscences by Miriam Gabo, Naum Gabo, Barbara Hepworth, Ben Nicholson, Winifred Nicholson, Herbert Read', *Studio International*, vol.172, Sept. 1966, pp.285–92.

Henkels, Herbert, 'Mondrian in seinem Atelier. Ein Essay über Mondrians Künstlertum/Mondriaan in zijn atelier. Een essay over Mondriaan's kunstenaarschap/ Mondrian in His Studio: Mondrian's Vision of Himself as Artist' in *Mondrian. Zeichnungen*, exh. cat., Staatsgalerie Stuttgart 1980, pp.219–85.

Henkels, Herbert, 'Introduction' and 'Mondrian: A Life in Pictures 1872–1944' in *Mondrian*, exh. cat., The Seibu Museum of Art, Tokyo 1987, pp.33–40, 192–235.

Holtzman, Harry, introduction to *Piet Mondrian: Plastic Art and Pure Plastic Art 1937 and Other Essays, 1941–1943*, ed. Robert Motherwell, New York 1945.

Harry Holtzman and Martin James, *The New Art – The New Life: The Collected Writings of Piet Mondrain*, Boston 1986.

Jaffé, Hans Ludwig, *De Stijl: 1917–1931. The Dutch Contribution to Modern Art*, Amsterdam and Brighton 1956.

Jaffé, H.L.C., *Piet Mondrian*, New York and London 1970.

'Harriet and Sidney Janis on Mondrian' in *Mondrian in the Sidney Janis Family Collections, New York*, exh.cat., Haags Gemeentemuseum, The Hague 1988, pp.7–22.

Joosten, Joop, 'Mondrian: Between Cubism and Abstraction' in *Piet Mondrian: Centennial Exhibition*, exh. cat., The Solomon R. Guggenheim Museum, New York 1971, pp.53–66.

Joosten, Joop, 'Mondrians verlorene Skizzenbücher aus den Jahren 1911–1914/ Mondriaans verloren gegane schetsboeken uit de jaren 1911 tot en met 1914/Mondrian's Lost Sketch-Books from the Years 1911–1914' in *Mondrian. Zeichnungen*, exh. cat., Stattsgalerie Stuttgart, 1980, pp.63–73.

Lissitzky, El, and Hans Arp, *Die Kunstismen | Les ismes de l'art | The Isms of Art, 1924–1914*, Erlenbach, Munich and Leipzig 1925.

Lohse, Richard P., 'Standard, Series, Module: New Problems and Tasks of Painting' in *Module, Proportion, Symmetry, Rhythm*, ed. Gyorgy Kepes, New York 1966, pp.130–6.

Moholy-Nagy, L., *Vision in Motion*, 2nd ed., Chicago 1947.

Ottolenghi, Maria Grazia, *L'opera completa di Mondrian*, Classici dell'Arte 77, Milan 1974.

Oud, J.J.P., 'Mondrian, de mens' in L.J.F. Wijsenbeek and J.J.P. Oud, *Mondriaan*, Zeist and Antwerp 1962, pp.61–81.

Ozenfant, Amédée, and Charles Edouard Jeanneret, *La Peinture moderne*, Paris 1925.

Paintings of the Rijksmuseum Kröller-Müller, compiled by F.Th. Gribling and P.H. Hefting, 3rd ed., Otterlo 1969; Dutch ed. 1970.

Rosenblum, Robert, *Cubism and Twentieth-Century Art*, New York 1961.

Rosenblum, Robert, 'Mondrian's Late Style' lecture given at the 'Old Age' Symposium, 14–15 January 1977, *Allen Memorial Art Museum Bulletin*, vol.35, 1977, pp.68–77.

Rowell, Margit, 'Interview with Charmion von Weigand, June 20, 1971' in *Piet Mondrian: Centennial Exhibition*, exh. cat., The Solomon R. Guggenheim Museum, New York 1971, pp.77–85.

Schapiro, Meyer, 'Mondrian: Order and Randomness in Abstract Painting' in *Modern Art: 19th and 20th Century. Selected Papers*, New York 1978, pp.233–61.

Seuphor, Michel, *Piet Mondrian: Life and Work*, New York, London and Amsterdam [1956].

Mondrian, introduction and biography by Michel Seuphor, exh. cat., Orangerie des Tuileries, Paris 1969.

Sweeney, James Johnson, 'Piet Mondrian' *The Museum of Modern Art Bulletin*, vol.12 Spring 1945, pp.2–12.

Sweeney, James Johnson, 'Eleven Europeans in America', *The Museum of Modern Art Bulletin*, vol.13, September 1946, pp.35–37; reprinted in Sweeney, *Piet Mondrian*, New York 1948, pp.15–16.

Sylvester, David, *Modern Art: From Fauvism to Abstract Expressionism*, New York 1965.

Trot, Nancy J., 'Mondrian's Designs for the "Salon de Madame B ... à Dresden"', *The Art Bulletin*, vol.72, December 1980, pp.640–7.

van Doesburg, Theo, 'Aanteekeningen bij twee teekeningen van Piet Mondriaan', *De Stijl* vol.1, no.9, July 1918, pp.108–11.

van Doesburg, Theo, 'Grondbegrippen der nieuwe beeldende kunst', *Tijdschrift voor Wijsbegeerte*, vol.13, April 1919, pp.180–1, 186–7.

Vantongerloo, G., 'L'Art plastique [L2]=[s] Néo-Plasticisme', *Vouloir*, vol.22, 1926, n.p.

von Maur, Karin, 'Musikalische Strukturen in der Kunst des 20. Jahrhunderts' and 'Mondrian und die Musik im "Stijl"' in *Vom Klang der Bilder*, exh. cat., Staatsgalerie Stuttgart 1985, pp.18–19, 400–7.

von Weigand, Charmion, 'The Meaning of Mondrian' *Journal of Aesthetics and Art Criticism*, vol.2, Fall 1943, pp.62–70.

von Weigand, Charmion, 'Mondrian: A Memoir of his New York Period', *Arts Yearbook*, vol.4, 1961, pp.57–65.

Welsh, Robert P., 'Mondrian and Theosophy' in *Piet Mondrian: Centennial Exhibition*, exh. cat., The Solomon R. Guggenheim Museum, New York 1971, pp.35–51.

Welsh, Robert P., 'Theo van Doesburg and Geometric Abstraction' in *Nijhoff, Van Ostaijen, 'De Stijl.' Modernism in The Netherlands and Belgium in the First Quarter of the 20th Century*, ed. Francis Bulhof, The Hague 1976, pp.76–94.

Welsh, Robert P., *Piet Mondrian's Early Career: The 'Naturalistic' Periods*. Ph.D. dissertation, Princeton University 1965, New York and London 1977.

Welsh, Robert P., 'The Place of "Composition 12 with Small Blue Square" in the Art of Piet Mondrian', *Bulletin of the National Gallery of Canada*, vol.29, 1977, pp.3–33.

Welsh, Robert P., 'Mondrian als Zeichner / Mondriaan als tekenaar / Mondrian as Draftsman' in *Mondrian. Zeichnungen*, exh. cat., Staatsgalerie Stuttgart 1980, pp.35–62.

Welsh, Robert P., and J.M. Joosten, *Two Mondrian Sketchbooks 1912–1914*, preface by Harry Holtzman, The Hague and Amsterdam 1969.

Weyergraf, Clara, *Piet Mondrian und Theo van Doesburg. Deutung von Werk und Theorie*, Munich 1979.

Wijsenbeek, L.J.F., 'Mondriaan. Schilder en denker' in L.J.F. Wijsenbeek and J.J.P. Oud, *Mondriaan*, Zeist and Antwerp 1962, pp.9–57.

LENDERS

British Museum, London 45

Private Collections 36, 69

The Scottish National Gallery of Modern Art, Edinburgh 66

Stedelijk Museum, Amsterdam 63

Tate Gallery, London 46, 60, 67

All other works lent by the Haags Gemeentemuseum, The Hague

PHOTOGRAPHIC CREDITS

Annely Juda Fine Art

British Museum, London

Gemeentearchief Amsterdam

Haags Gemeentemuseum, The Hague

David Heald © The Solomon R. Guggenheim Foundation, New York

Mark Heathcote

Kroller-Müller Museum, Otterlo

Marcus Leith

The Museum of Modern Art, New York

National Galleries of Scotland, Edinburgh

Cas Oorthtuys

Rijksmuseum Amsterdam

Giuseppe Schiavinotto

Stedelijk Museum, Amsterdam

Tate Gallery Photographic Department

Thomas Ammann Fine Art

Winterthur Kunstmuseum